During such challenging times for the Church, we need a clear and direct message of hope. Justin Fatica's orthodox message of Christ's love is delivered in a new and convincing way. Our Lord's marching order to the Apostles was, "Go and make disciples of all the nations." *Win It All* gives us hope. It shows the way for young people to become disciples of Christ and committed members of his Church.

Cardinal Seán O'Malley, O.F.M. Cap.
Archbishop of Boston

Justin Fatica is a faith-filled disciple of the Lord who has helped many young people to reclaim their faith. His sincerity and personal witness have energized many to deepen their love of God and live their discipleship.

Most Reverend Donald W. Trautman
Bishop of Erie

Faith, hope, and love are the virtues that help us to live in a close relationship with God: Father, Son, and Holy Spirit. Faith in God, hope for Heaven, love for all: these are what animate Justin Fatica. With deep passion, Justin shares this faith, hope, and love with young people, teaching and inspiring them to have a living relationship with the Holy Trinity. The new evangelization requires new evangelizers. Justin Fatica is indeed a new evangelizer, helping others to encounter Christ and the liberating truth of his Gospel.

Most Reverend Kevin C. Rhoades
Bishop of Fort Wayne-South Bend

Justin Fatica's passion for and commitment to Jesus Christ is evident on every page of *Win It All*. His book covers topics like mission, courage, love, and perseverance and his stories will resonate with the real life issues of young people. This is a journey that will appeal to our young people.

Bob McCarty
Executive Director
National Federation for Catholic Youth Ministry

Nobody is reaching Catholic teens like Justin Fatica. *Win It All* is another example of his commitment to helping today's youth discover the incredible life that God is inviting them to live. Give a copy to every teen you know.

Matthew Kelly
Author of *Rediscovering Catholicism*

Justin Fatica's love for and dedication to young people is obvious in his ministry, and he definitely reaches people who are often missed by other speakers.

Mike Norman
Office of Religious Education
Archdiocese of Los Angeles

Having shared a meal with Justin Fatica I can tell that his heart for ministry and young people is passionately genuine. He is an effective speaker and storyteller who will have a lasting impact on any diocese or parish that invites him in.

John M. Rinaldo
Director of Youth Ministry
Diocese of San Jose

God is doing great things through Justin Fatica. . . . Justin's honesty about his own life experiences and relationship with Jesus Christ connects with the students, and encourages them to come forward and give witness to a presence of Christ in their lives that they had not known or had misplaced.

Joseph Pounder
Director of Campus Ministry
Bishop Ludden Jr./Sr. High School

Win it All

THE WAY TO HEAVEN FOR CATHOLIC TEENS

JUSTIN FATICA

ave maria press AmP notre dame, indiana

Imprimatur: Most Reverend Robert J. Cunningham
            Bishop of Syracuse

Given at: Syracuse, NY, on 28 May 2010.

Founded in 1865, Ave Maria Press is a ministry of the Indiana Province of Holy Cross.

www.avemariapress.com

ISBN-10 1-59471-249-2   ISBN-13 978-1-59471-249-4

Cover image © Konrad Mostert/stock.xchng.

Cover and text design by Andy Wagoner.

Printed and bound in the United States of America.

Library of Congress Cataloging-in-Publication Data

Fatica, Justin.
  Win it all : the way to heaven for Catholic teens / Justin Fatica.
     p. cm.
  ISBN-13: 978-1-59471-249-4 (pbk.)
  ISBN-10: 1-59471-249-2 (pbk.)
  1. Catholic teenagers--Religious life. 2. Spiritual formation--Catholic Church. I. Title.
  BX2355.F38 2010
  248.8'3088282--dc22
                                        2010025970

Contents

Foreword

Sometimes in life God allows us to reexamine where we have been in order to adjust where it is we are going. What are we dreaming about, longing for, and striving to become? What unhealthy fears do we clutch, which keeps us from becoming better persons? Occasionally we'll read a phrase that catches our attention or challenges us in some way, but most of the time, God brings us a real-life person to shake us out of our comfort zone, remind us of our dreams, and assist us over our fears. In ways, Justin Fatica has been that "holy shake" in my life.

We like to compartmentalize other people. This person is a Democrat, that one is a Republican. Maybe this started when we were younger, noticing that over here are the jocks while over there are the emo kids and the geeks. This labeling, unfortunately, happens even within ministry. Why? Because it is so much easier to stereotype another or make quick judgments about a person than it is to actually find out what truly makes another tick. People are messy, and by putting them into a quick box we can move on with our lives without getting to know each other. It's safer that way. But God doesn't want us to be safe. Rather, he wants us to be saints!

The first time I met Justin eight years ago, he was carrying a baseball bat. No joke! We were in Yardley, Pennsylvania, doing a ministry event together, and I can honestly say I was shocked with his prop and even more so with his presentation. Who was this guy? Yes, he was in perfect physical shape (grumble, grumble), had no body fat (complain, sigh), and was fearless in presenting the Gospel. But ministry by baseball bat?

It would have been so easy to categorize Justin as a person who presented Christ in a manner that was too confrontational than to actually get to know him. That night his talk was passionate and zealous. Still I wondered if he really cared about the kids—or was it all a gimmick?

Later that evening I felt that holy shake as we talked about ministry and family. You see, I found out that Justin loves not only his wife and kids, but he also loves *all* people! Justin has a special interest in those individuals with innumerable flaws. Because Justin's own life was messy, he wasn't afraid of the mess in the lives of others. I've gotten to know that Justin loves enough to say the things that most of us would never imagine saying. He can be a little unnerving because of his style and presentation.

Because of his boldness, Justin has probably been compartmentalized by others in ministry more than anyone else. But I believe he thinks of this as a good thing because as a result, I think he has probably spent more time reexamining where he's been and where he is going in ministry than many others have. Somewhere along the line, Justin decided that he would care more about souls than opportunities to settle into any "in" group. That has really impressed me.

The holy shake I have received from Justin has helped me as I looked at my own ministry. Have there been times where I was reserved in my presentation because I wanted to be invited back into the school, parish, or conference? Have there been times I tickled ears instead of presenting the Gospel without restriction? I hope not. The message of the cross still causes many to stumble and often seems foolish to others, but the Good News of Christ cannot be presented with any restrictions or reservations.

Justin's new book, *Win It All: The Way to Heaven for Catholic Teens*, will shake you up! Justin gives eight steps to help teens become faithful disciples and, in reality, saints. The message in *Win It All* is for all of us who have a messy life. Justin's words cut to the quick, but many of our beloved saints spoke that way as well.

Some of the saints decided that preaching the Gospel was more important than anything the world could offer. Is Justin a saint? He can be, and so can you, but you can be sure it won't happen by accident. It certainly will not happen by labeling another, holding back because of fear, or worrying if your way is in sync with the cultural norm. Justin knows teenagers, and he is aware that they are willing to be challenged toward greatness. The language Justin uses is familiar to this generation of youth; he says what they think and can hear what they say, which is such a need for authentic dialogue. Whereas many might pass by the girl at the restaurant table who looks sad and despondent, Justin invites her to sit next to him. In this book, Justin tells what happened when he did that. He shows what happens when we truly look at those along this journey and actually love them. That is what Justin is doing. I pray that is what you and I are doing. I think *Win It All: The Way to Heaven for Catholic Teens* is a resource to help us all to do better.

Chris Padgett
Christian Speaker and Worship Leader
March 2010

Introduction

I sit here late at night in Columbia, a small rural town close to the University of South Carolina, thinking about my day.

At 6:30 a.m., I woke up to walk and pray, and the only warm place I could think to go to was the Waffle House down the street from my hotel. I ordered some instant grits and eggs, and then I began to read the Bible in prayer. Nearby, some waitresses were talking, joking, and having fun. After I said my prayers, I started to put a talk together for later that night. It was called "Give It All You Got." I looked over, and there was a young waitress staring down into her coffee cup. She had her coat on, and I assumed that she was waiting for her ride

1

home after working the night shift. I heard her sniffle and saw that she was crying.

I said to her, "Hey, come sit over here." I wasn't sure if she understood my East Coast accent, so I said it again: "Come sit with me." She didn't waste any time. She came over to my table and sat down with tears in her eyes. I asked her what was wrong, but she wouldn't say. I turned to my book *Hard as Nails*, a book written with stories and letters from people I have met throughout my early years of ministry. I opened to a page with a title that read, "I am abandoned." She looked down at the title and said, "Yes, that's me." She wiped away her tears.

I asked her, "So what are you going through?" She started crying harder and told me, "I'm just very lonely." After introducing herself as Christine, she went on to say that she was also afraid of losing her job. I told her I was sorry for what she was going through but to remember that her life was truly valuable and important. I gave her my book and told her to keep in touch by e-mail so that I could remind her how very important she is.

I had come to the Waffle House to pray, eat, and get ready for my talk. But all that was put on hold because real life got in the way. And thankfully I realized what takes priority in life. Sometimes God guides you to the Waffle House to reach out to those who are in need of love. In my years ministering to thousands of teenagers, I have learned that it's about loving them all today, not tomorrow.

The title of this book is *Win It All: The Way to Heaven for Catholic Teens*. Usually when you hear a phrase like "win it all," it has something to do with gaining a victory in a game or accumulating more money, possessions, and fame than the next person. That is not what I mean by winning it all. Surely, there is a goal and prize involved, but the one I am speaking about in this book is the one of greatest value. The goal of winning it all is Heaven, plain and simple. In eight steps, I will encourage, cajole, and remind you to put everything else in your life in second place—like I did with my immediate tasks at the Waffle House—to focus on what it takes to achieve that goal for yourself, your family, your friends, and even your enemies.

Of course, the secret to Heaven has nothing to do with any number of steps. It has to do with Jesus Christ, who by his death on a cross won our redemption and opened the possibility that we can live forever. This book shouts out praise to the Lord. It also is filled with inspirational stories of saints from the past and heroes from the present who have put their faith in him before all else. It shares a roadmap for living out these steps that takes place in the Catholic Church, especially through participation in the sacraments.

If we want to win it all for ourselves and others, people like Christine at the Waffle House need us to jump on board the mission with Jesus Christ. We need to realize that winning it all involves giving it our all every day, all day. Each day, people like Christine need us, and we need to dig down deep and keep our passion for the gospel of Jesus Christ alive. Don't be afraid.

We can't get caught up in the small stuff the media bombards us with each day. We can't even make sports, school, entertainment, or work more important than reaching out in love to others. We can't get caught up in ourselves. Instead, we must focus on reaching out to people and sharing our love for the Lord and our commitment to his Church. This isn't a task for tomorrow. They need us TODAY! We need to commit to loving with all our hearts and souls. Fr. Larry Richards, my mentor, shared this winning formula, JOY:

- Love Jesus first.
- Love Others second.
- Love Yourself third.

Every day, the people around me reaffirm my faith and my drive to win Heaven. Have you ever kept running into someone and wondered why? I keep running into Mr. Lynch, a seventy-year-old man with faith and wisdom. We've become friends because we keep seeing each other unexpectedly, and I talk to him whenever I see him. I think we are meant to meet up like we have so that we can encourage each other and share our stories.

I walked into Doug's Fish Fry on a cold January day in upstate New York, and there he was again. We talked for a little while as he was eating lunch and reading the newspaper. I told him that I have been praying for him since his wife died. I had to leave soon, but my heart told me to ask him a question first: "If you could give me only one message today, what would it be?"

With a tender heart and a look of compassion, he said, "When life kicks you in the pants, how will you react? It's bound to happen. Everyone gets kicked in the pants. But how will you deal with it, Justin? That is what's important."

I thought to myself, I know from my own experience how to respond to what Mr. Lynch just said. I know from the gospel. I know from the Church. I felt like shouting back to Mr. Lynch (but I didn't!), "I WILL WIN IT ALL!" I will follow Jesus Christ and live in the Church. I will put the eight steps of this book into daily practice.

We all face challenges, we all get kicked in the pants sometimes, and it is important that we have a rock-solid foundation of faith to support us.

So come on this journey with me. Reading this book will help you be true to your core foundation as Catholic Christians who love and follow the Lord.

You will not fail, even if life kicks you in the pants. No matter what happens, God is with us, and we will win!

one[1]

Recognize Your Importance

YOU ARE AMAZING!

It was a crowded Saturday afternoon at the mall. I was in a hurry, and so was everyone else. I had a few packages in my hands, and I balanced them as I looked down to catch my footing on the escalator leaving the food court. I was heading downstairs to ground level, a quick turn right, and then out the door to the parking garage. I was glad to be about to escape this shopping madness.

When I finally looked up, I noticed a man out of the corner of my eye. You couldn't miss him. He was sitting in close proximity to the fast food. A mess surrounded him. There were three-ring binders and notebooks of all kinds. They were not neat at all. Papers were hanging out the edges. He was disheveled too—one side of his shirt hung untucked. He was a big guy—I guessed he weighed more than three hundred pounds.

I don't know what struck me about this man. But my heart was pounding. I am seriously ADHD myself, and I felt one of those bursts of active energy. I needed to reach out to this man. Even with all his rumpled papers and his unkempt appearance, or maybe because of them, I knew this man was special.

I turned around at the bottom of the escalator and headed back to the second level and the food court. I watched him for a minute as he unpacked his stuff. He went to one of the counters and ordered a large bowl of soup and carefully carried it back to his table on a tray. While he was waiting for the soup to cool off, I approached and sat across from him.

"I just want to say that you are amazing," I began.

"What did you say?" I said it again, only louder: "YOU ARE AMAZING!"

"Are you sure?"

He was definitely shocked and confused, and I wasn't altogether sure that he wasn't about to reach across the table, grab me by the collar, and shake me. I have that effect on people even when I say positive stuff.

"Can I sit with you and explain myself?" I went on.

"Okay."

The man's name is Andrew. He had all of those papers because he is a writer. In fact, he has worked on several of the *Chicken Soup for the Soul* books. He is practically an expert on the ins and outs of book publishing. In the course of our conversation, I learned more about publishing from Andrew than I have from anyone ever since. Without Andrew, I would have had no clue as to how to go about getting my first book, *Hard as Nails*, into print and published by one of the largest publishers.

I found out in sitting with Andrew that day that I was right: he is amazing!

Of course, he wanted to know about me and why I was at his table. I told him it was a long story, but one way to sum it up was like this: "I have a Father in Heaven who loves me more than I know. He thinks I am important just because of the way I am. And he asks me to recognize the importance of others."

Andrew looked a little shocked. I wasn't sure if he still thought I was a bit crazy. But he didn't ask me to leave. And we remain friends today. As a postscript, I have to also tell you that Andrew has lost more than one hundred pounds and continues to make a difference in the lives of others through his gift of writing.

YOU ARE LOVED!

Because of my faith, I reached out to Andrew and told him he was important. The only reason I thought he needed to hear this message from me is that everyone needs to hear how important, unique, and special he or she is. You need to hear it, too: God has made you as a one-and-only you. When God looks at you, he sees you with the pride of a Father who has made you irreplaceable to him. Our main problem is that we don't always remember how important we are.

When God's Son, Jesus Christ, came to earth, this was the same message he told over and over. On one occasion, Jesus pointed out the birds in the sky to his disciples. "Notice the ravens: they do not sow or reap; they have neither storehouse nor barn, yet God feeds them. How much more important are you than birds?" (Lk 12:24).

Did you hear what Jesus was saying in these words? The birds don't have a prestigious job or special title like *farmer*. Yet God loves and cares for them.

How often do we think that we are only loveable based on what we do or what we produce? I used to think like that at your age.

I used to wonder how I would measure up to all of the accomplishments of my parents. I didn't think I could. So you know what I did? I did the opposite. Because I connected my importance only with what I could produce, I began to produce nothing. I did a lot of dumb things.

I grew up in Erie, Pennsylvania, where there are a lot of small creeks. Probably some of the dumbest things I ever did was to light a few of those creeks on fire. You might be wondering how anyone can do that. With a group of my friends, who were also not too bright, we would pour gasoline in a creek, strike a match, and watch the creek literally blow up in front of our eyes. But soon that wasn't enough. We decided to run through the fire.

A few of my friends went first. They ran through to the other side. There was a lot of whooping and cheering. My intensity was rising. I had to do it, too! Only I was even dumber than they were. When I had reached the middle of the fire I could see my friends' expressions go from giddy to shocked to scared. What could it be? And then I realized I was still carrying the gasoline can.

I exploded. I was on fire. Thank goodness that in second grade I learned about "stop, drop, and roll." And let me tell you it does work. My friends patted me down and somehow kept me from cooking myself to death.

But in my mind there was something worse than being on fire. I had lost my dad's gasoline can. My dad is one of those people who is obsessive-compulsive to the point that every tool in his garage had to be in place. He would certainly notice the missing gas can.

I am a bad liar. Nevertheless, I tried to lie, and I told him "I don't know" when he asked me where the gasoline can was. He noticed that I was smirking, and it didn't take much prodding for him to question me to the point where I admitted that I had set the creek, my friends, and myself on fire.

Now I have to tell you an even dumber thing. Because I thought of myself as invincible even though my self-worth was actually really low, I decided to do it again. One week later, I was back on the creek lighting fires again. And this time I didn't run through the fire. I walked. I was on fire again. What was I doing to myself? My clothes were damaged, and my face was seared.

The next morning my dad was hanging out with my friends. I remember we were watching *SportsCenter* and eating our Lucky Charms. My friends may have been enjoying themselves, but I was worried about what I would say to my dad. I figured he was going to find out, so I might as well go down with my boys nearby. So I said to my dad, "I set myself on fire again."

My friends were laughing so hard that marshmallows from the cereal were flying out of their mouths. My dad didn't seem to have heard me. So I repeated, "Dad, I did it again."

"What did you do again?"

"I lit myself on fire in the creek, and I lost your gasoline can."

My dad was both shocked and perplexed. He glanced toward my friends, who nodded as if to say, "Yep, he did it again."

From across the room my dad said simply, "Come here."

He screamed some at me and told me what I had done was stupid. "You don't understand how dangerous that was. That could have killed you." But even while all of the yelling was going on I had a very real sense that he still loved me and that he was saying all he said because he cared about me.

YOU ARE IMPORTANT!

The way my father reacted gave me a glimpse of God's love and care for us. By thinking I had to *do* something to possess my parents' love, I was incorrect. My dad wanted the best for me and for me to be safe. Can you imagine how much more Father in Heaven loves you and will continue to love you no matter what "bad" thing you might do? Think about this: God loves you even if you have struggled with destructive behaviors like using alcohol or drugs, risking your physical and emotional well-being by having sex before marriage, or even cutting yourself and trying to end your life. God cares. God doesn't stop caring.

Likewise, your worth in God's eyes is not based on any storehouse or barn of possessions. In your world today so much emphasis is placed on what things you have acquired— not just possessions that can be purchased with money, but also things like membership in the "right" group of friends to chill with, power over another in a relationship, prestige for the way our bodies look, instead of focusing on who we really are. It's not about how "hot" you are or how high your "ranking" is in the world. God's message is this: You are important for who you are, not for what you do or what you own! I love you no matter what!

God says to us the same words he spoke to the prophet Jeremiah in the Old Testament: "Before I formed you in the womb I knew you" (Jer 1:5). The Lord has known us since the beginning of time that is, before our conception, before we came into being. If you have been baptized, you have actually been sealed by God and given to Christ as one who belongs to him forever. You all see people with tattoos. You may have one yourself. Well, you have been "tattooed" with the mark of Christ. It is a permanent mark that will never go away. Let that sink in. There is nothing you can do or not do that would keep God from loving you.

When you recognize your importance and never forget it, you can have a great effect on others. By the time I had met Andrew at the mall, if I was not confident in my own importance, do you think I would have been able to approach and affirm Andrew? I don't think so. Other people need us. We can help them only if we don't forget who we are as sons or daughters of a loving Father.

WHAT DOES JESUS TEACH?

Do you know the story of Zacchaeus from the Gospel of Luke?

Zacchaeus was someone who forgot his importance. He was a Jew, born into God's Chosen People, and taught in the ways of God. But he had fallen off that course. He had gone to work for the Roman occupiers who had forced the Jews to pay taxes to Caesar, the emperor. Zacchaeus not only went to his Jewish neighbors to collect the taxes, he was skimming some money off for himself, too.

Zacchaeus was also a little man. I mean he was physically small. (He was probably like me. My good friend David Tyree calls me an Italian midget!) Could Zacchaeus's short stature have damaged the way he felt about himself? We don't know for sure. But we do know that he stayed out of the way when Jesus came to his hometown of Jericho. The Gospel says that because of his size he couldn't see Jesus along the route. Instead,

> He ran ahead and climbed a sycamore tree in order to see Jesus, who was about to pass that way. When he reached the place, Jesus looked up and said to him, "Zacchaeus, come down quickly, for today I must stay at your house." And he came down quickly and received him with joy. (Lk 19:4–6)

Win it All

Jesus' opponents didn't appreciate that Jesus had recognized a sinner. They didn't like it that Jesus was going to eat at Zaccahaeus's house. But what happens when someone recognizes the God-given importance of another? That person, newly affirmed, wants to share this gift with others, too! That's what Zacchaeus wanted to do. He said to Jesus so that everyone could hear:

> "Behold, half of my possessions, Lord, I shall give to the poor, and if I have extorted anything from anyone I shall repay it four times over." And Jesus said to him, "Today salvation has come to this house because this man too is a descendant of Abraham." (Lk 19:8–10)

Don't ever forget the lessons that Jesus' meeting with Zacchaeus teach us. Here are a few:

1. *When we forget our importance, we do things that oppose who we really are.* Zacchaeus cheated his Jewish relatives. I tried to destroy myself by walking through a fire.

2. *Our physical appearances don't have anything to do with how loveable we are in God's eyes.* Zacchaeus climbed a tree, not only to be able to see Jesus, but to make sure that Jesus did not see him. Jesus saw beyond the limbs and branches and leaves. He found Zacchaeus and affirmed him. He forgave Zacchaeus's sins and called him to be even better. At first, I noticed my friend Andrew because he seemed lonely and in need of encouragement. But once I started to know Andrew, I moved well beyond skin and pounds and soup spilled on his shirt. (Yes, he had that, too, at our first meeting!)

I had approached Andrew and told him he was "amazing." But the real affirmation came in reverse. Andrew recognized my importance through my self-doubt and told me a way that I could really go about having my story published in a book. Only with his help was I able to do that.

3. *Others may not believe that we can change our lives.* When some of the people saw that Jesus was going to stay with Zacchaeus, they began to grumble. Have you ever known people who did not want you to improve your life? Maybe you have quit partying, and some of those who are still hanging out and drinking don't appreciate your change. Why is this so? Do you think some people want to keep you down because it makes them feel better about themselves? In these cases it might be best to tell them of their importance, too. They are capable of changing just like you.

4. *When we know our own importance, we can help others to know theirs.* Jesus, God-Made-Flesh, never forgot his place as the Son of a loving Father. In knowing that, he was able to reach out to sinners. In fact, this was his mission. He tells Zacchaeus and the others this: "For the Son of Man has come to seek and to save what was lost" (Lk 19:10).

SHARE YOURSELF WITH OTHERS

I am reminded of the lesson of being able to translate our positive knowledge of our importance to help others every time I travel around the country preaching to teenagers and witnessing how they are transformed by the good news of Jesus Christ. And I have a friend, Britney, who reminds me of this all of the time. A few years ago after I returned from the road, I opened an e-mail from Britney that told her story.

> My parents got divorced when I was little and shared custody. At first there were no problems, and everything remained civil. Both of my parents got remarried. My sister and I lived with my mom and stepdad. We both knew that he was abusive to her. We just didn't know how bad and all of the reasons why.
>
> One summer when I was thirteen, I took a trip to California. When I returned home, I found out my mother was in jail. She had been using and selling cocaine. She was addicted.
>
> At first she promised me that she would get help. But she didn't. Things only got worse. She let my stepfather back in the house for about the hundredth time. I couldn't take watching the abuse, so I went to live with my dad.
>
> About the same time, I started dating a guy who I really liked. When he broke up with me, I went off the deep end. Why couldn't I make any relationship work? That is when I tried to kill myself. I took about thirty aspirin and passed out.
>
> From that lowest of lows I heard your message: You are important because of the way God made you. Return to God. Recognize who you really are.

I think about Britney and her story a lot. I am humbled that the Hard as Nails ministry and I were able to help her. But I also wonder what would have happened to Britney if we weren't there to affirm her and proclaim her goodness. And believe me, I wouldn't have been in any position to help anyone if those many years ago I hadn't heard God calling to me to help me recognize that I am important because of the way God made *me!* Thank God! Praise God!

And I have to add: Britney now travels with our Hard as Nails ministry team and helps others who have experienced divorce, drugs, abuse, depression, and so many other types of pain that none of us can escape.

As Catholics we are intertwined and interconnected. Our Baptism makes us so. It is Baptism that grounds us in our common mission to be holy and in the mission of sharing the good news with others. Baptism is the sacrament of regeneration and renewal by the Holy Spirit:

> Through Baptism we are freed from sin and reborn as sons of God; we become members of Christ; and are incorporated into the Church and made sharers in her mission. (*Catechism of the Catholic Church*, 1213)

This means that as my dad reached out in love and compassion to me, I reached out in a crowded mall to Andrew, and Andrew, filled with God's grace, affirmed and shared himself with me. It means that a hurt and broken child named Britney heard the message that she was loved and special, made that message the core of her life, and now shares it again and again with teenagers who are as broken as she once was.

Remember that you are important. Please!

Never forget how much the Creator God loves you!

Win ^it All

Questions to Help You Win It All

1. Why does God love me so much?

2. How can I express my real self to others?

3. Who is someone I see every day that needs to be affirmed?

STEPS TO RECOGNIZE YOUR IMPORTANCE

- Write letters of affirmation to a family member, friend, and a classmate you never speak with. Tell each person what you notice about him or her that screams to the world of his or her importance. Put a stamp on your letter and send it through the mail.

- Create an intercessory prayer list of all those who have made an everlasting impact on your life *and* other people who you feel don't know how important they are. Start a regular time of praying for everyone on your list.

- Take five minutes a day to sit and listen to God. Ask God to tell you about how much he loves the one and only you. (See Five-Minute Prayer on page 140.)

two²

Discover Your Mission in Life

OPEN TO LIFE

Let me cut to the chase and get right to the heart of the message for Step 2: If you are teenager growing into adulthood and *not* open to making a commitment to being a priest, religious sister or brother, a faithful spouse in marriage, or living a single life with a strong dedication to others, then you will not understand what it means to discover the mission for your life.

These vocations, or callings—priesthood, religious life, marriage, and committed single life—are the ways Catholics live out their lives.

Win it All

Let's take another leap of faith before we move on: While most people do, in fact, eventually marry, it is important for you and for the Church that you consider the vocations of the ordained priesthood if you are a male and the consecrated life as a sister if you are a female. Don't dismiss this invitation to explore these vocations. Don't think these callings could never be for you. I know a young man named Paul who seemed the least likely person to be a priest. As I write this, he is just months away from his ordination as a deacon, a transitional step before he is ordained a priest.

I met Paul in the fall of 2000 when he was a senior at Paramus Catholic High School in New Jersey. This was the time when a freshman approached Paul and said to him, "You pretty much own this school, don't you?" Paul ate up that message. He told me that from a young age he always had a desire for some kind of fame.

Really, Paul's resumé was becoming more and more infamous. He was kicked out of the local middle school for displaying a bag of marijuana that turned out to be oregano. His active drug use escalated, and he ended up in Narcotics Anonymous, where he put a stop to that addiction only to translate his addictive personality to a pattern of being controlling in his relationships with girlfriends.

After a girl he cared deeply about left him, Paul broke down crying in class and then ended up in the office of a consoling priest who invited him on a school retreat. It was then that he began to change his life.

But not all of the way. After he graduated from high school, Paul's new road to fame was as a comedian, and he landed an act in New York City. He invited me and my future wife, Mary, to see him perform. We went to the comedy club and heard jokes that spewed swear words and sexual innuendoes.

"What do you think?" Paul wondered after the show.

"Paul, that was *pagan*," I told him. We laughed at the time, but Paul came to see me at Paramus a few days later. He asked me what I really meant by "pagan."

I explained that I didn't think he knew who he was really all about. All of these "other Pauls" were just acts. Paul continued to visit me, and we started hanging out. He was having more trouble in his relationships with girls. He was hurting inside.

Paul kept asking me questions. Hundreds of them. It wasn't long before the questions were mostly about religion, faith, and Jesus Christ.

Through the grace of the Holy Spirit, when Paul learned more about Jesus and developed a deeper friendship with the Lord, things finally changed quite drastically for him. Paul was baptized as a baby and had received the other sacraments of initiation. But in April 2004 Paul made a commitment to Jesus that he would live his life for him. By 2005, he had decided to enter the seminary and pursue priesthood.

One of the things Paul realized in coming to this decision was that he was not going to have to "give up" some of the unique and positive things that made him who he was. He could even be a "comedian priest" or a "rapper priest," which is in his heart to do one day. As a priest, he could be a lawyer, a doctor, or a teacher like some priests I know.

God gives us so much freedom to follow him in our own ways. Personally, I am a father and a husband. I am also an evangelist, a sports team motivator, an author, and a business leadership speaker. In the future, I could be a football coach or a blimp pilot! Who knows? While the things I do could change, my mission to love God will never change. This is a mission I share with each of you.

What I do know is that Paul and I share a common mission to love God with all our hearts, minds, souls, and strength and to love others as Christ would love them. This is where I want our common vocations—yours and mine—to intersect as you search out the unique and specific way you will follow the Lord.

HEAR GOD CALLING YOU

Now I'd like to tell you a story about a man named Charles de Foucald. He was a guy who was born rich, a lot like me. My parents have a lot of money. If you ever saw my parents' house on the HBO documentary about my life, you saw their mansion on Lake Erie. They also have a house in Key West on the Atlantic Ocean. I was sometimes embarrassed by all of the money they had, but it definitely affected who I am. They gave me a Jeep Wrangler before I was sixteen. I had an attitude that it was all about me. Charles de Foucald was like that: someone who was born rich but died poor. Or was that the other way around? Let me explain.

Charles was born in 1858 to an aristocratic family in France. Both of his parents died when he was very young, and they left Charles and his sister a large inheritance. For years afterward, Charles was indulged by the wealth. As he grew to adulthood, he enjoyed the finest foods and champagne to the point of being overweight.

All of this partying eventually made Charles bored. What else could he do for excitement, he wondered? In 1858, he entered the French army as an officer. He continued to brag about his extravagance and his arrogance. He took up with a mistress and flaunted his relationship with her at social functions, where the other officers and their wives were not amused by his public immoral behavior. Charles wouldn't listen to their criticism, and he resigned from the army.

Now rich and retired and barely thirty years old, Charles still had little concept of what he was really supposed to do with his life. He began to travel on expeditions through the oases of South Algeria and Tunisia and into Morocco. Because the French were not trusted in these areas, Charles pretended he was a Jew. In the desert Charles met Jews and Muslims, but no Christians. Though raised a Catholic, Charles hadn't even considered his faith, or God for that matter, in years.

This was about to change. Charles couldn't believe it when he saw a Muslim stop in the desert, unroll a rug, and bow in prayer to God. The faithfulness of his Jewish companions was also impressive. What was it with these people, he wondered? Their faith did not provide them with any material comforts, but it did seem to provide them with a resolve that allowed them to face all kinds of suffering and persecution.

These examples led Charles to pause and take a much deeper look at his life. He began to think about God and the Catholic faith. He returned to France and went off to pray on his knees for long hours each day at St. Augustine's Church. He kept repeating what he called his "strange prayer": "My God, if you exist, make your presence known to me."

Charles heard God's voice. He gave himself over to God's will. His life would take several more twists and turns, but from then on, they were done in the knowledge that he was God's special child. He was important to God, and his life had meaning. Around the time of this conversion, Charles wrote this prayer:

> Father,
> I abandon myself into your hands: do with me
>   what you will.
> Whatever you may do I thank you:
> I am ready for all, I accept all.
> Let only your will be done in me, and in all your
>   creatures—
> I wish no more than this, O Lord.
> Into your hands I commend my soul;
> I offer it to you with all the love of my heart,
> for I love you, Lord, and so need to give myself
> to surrender myself into your hands
> without reserve,
> and with boundless confidence,
> for you are my Father.

The title of this book is *Win It All*. What do you think it means to win it all? I'll tell you one thing it means: to win it all means to discover what God intends for our lives. The Father has a special plan for each of us. Once we remember how really important and special and one-of-a-kind we are to God, like Charles, we are compelled to find out what he wants us to do with our lives. We are to discover our mission in life. Then we can truly pursue or own personal vocation to serve the mission.

We "win it all" when we follow the will of God. We win it all when our mission is to love God with all our hearts, souls, and minds.

Jesus was not about earthly results. He had only three people at his funeral! Jesus cared more about the ultimate purpose of his mission than the immediate results. Jesus' desire was that people would be saved from their sins and reach eternal life in the company of the angels, saints, and Blessed Trinity—Father, Son, and Holy Spirit. Jesus' time on earth was more focused on effort and commitment, drive and mission. Your mission in life is to give it all you've got in quest of the ultimate prize—Heaven.

I truly believe that I am living God's will as a husband, father, and evangelist for the gospel. I feel truly alive whenever I share the good news that Jesus Christ is my Savior! Jesus Christ is Risen! Jesus Christ calls you to God's Kingdom! How good it is to do God's will. There is no better gift than putting Christ first in your life!

You are younger. You may not be certain of the vocation that God is calling you on for your entire life. But today you *can* discover right now what your mission is. Only then can you can begin to discover how that mission will unfold into a vocation and career. How do you do that? Begin with your passions.

WHAT MOVES YOU?

When the University of Notre Dame announced its new football coach, Brian Kelly, a sports writer asked him what kind of players he would like to have play for him. The coach didn't even hesitate. "I want players with passion. I want players who love to play football. I don't want anyone who is playing for any other reason except that they love to play. I don't want them to play on our team because their girlfriends want to date football players."

Keep the coach's words in mind as you begin to think more specifically about what will be your mission in life. What is it in your life now that makes your heart skip a beat? What do you have a passion for?

You might be able to put your finger on your passions by asking yourself:

- What am I good at?
- What do I like to do?

Typically, your responses will then reveal some of your God-given skills in athletics, performing arts, music, and academics. These are very helpful for you as you begin to plan your life path. Your passions in these areas of what you are good at and what you like to do will lead you to a variety of different *career* paths.

But a career is different from a mission or vocation.

Your mission is a personal commitment you make.

Vocation is a little trickier. It is a word that literally means "calling." For Catholics, a vocation is a call to live out a commitment to Jesus Christ. There are a few different ways that Catholics live out their vocations.

For guys, one vocation is the priesthood. For women and men, too, another vocation is the consecrated or religious life. We have met so many young men like Paul in our Hard as Nails ministry who have accepted God's call to explore the vocation of priest and many other young women who have professed vows as sisters. I think what attracts these people to exploring these vocations more deeply in seminaries and convents are the examples of their families and the support of their peers. Family life that centers on Jesus, the Eucharist, and the Blessed Mother is a perfect recipe for a vocation to the priesthood or religious life.

What if you heard that one of your friends was thinking about becoming a priest or a nun? How would you react? Please support them in this courageous and radical choice. The typical goals of society are strongly aligned against these types of vocations. Who in their right mind would want to make commitments to poverty, chastity, and obedience, the world asks? Jesus was aware of this. He warned his disciples:

> If the world hates you, realize that it hated me first.
> If you belonged to the world, the world would love
> its own; but because you do not belong to the world,
> and I have chosen you out of the world, the world
> hates you. (Jn 15:18–19)

If you are considering a vocation to the priesthood or religious life yourself, take heart! Find support in those around you. You are considering a much-needed vocation for building up the Church and the Kingdom of God.

Catholics live out their commitment to Christ in two other main ways. Christian marriage is the most "popular" vocation. There is a very good chance that you will be married some day. You prepare for this vocation by the way you respect your body and forming healthy friendships with your peers, especially those of the opposite sex.

Let me explain this in a little more detail.

We need to always remember that our bodies are to be respected. I had not met my wife yet when I committed myself at age seventeen to save myself for her. This was a crucial and important decision for a seventeen-year-old to make and one for which I will always be thankful. When I made this promise, I was really beginning my commitment to my life-long vocation of marriage.

I could have never dreamed of receiving from God the wife he has given me. I often walk around the block in my neighborhood thanking God for the gift of my wife and my life. Thank you so much, Lord.

My good friend Jeff asked me before he got married for some words of advice. I told him, "Please remember what you sacrificed." People who have sacrificed very little for their vocation will not appreciate what they are given. I reminded Jeff that there were many other women who would have liked to marry him (or sleep with him before marriage) but that he had stayed the course and not given into the temptations of the flesh. He had saved himself specially for his bride, Whitney, whom he admired and loved. I also reminded Jeff that just as his commitment to Jesus Christ was forever, the same was true for his commitment to his wife.

Purity, sacrifice, admiration for your spouse, and commitment to Christ are what prepare you for and make a strong marriage.

As I grow older, I realize that my wife just keeps getting more beautiful. Her wisdom and heart will always be young. I committed to my wife because she will help me to get to Heaven. Many times we are weak on our own to win it all. The vocation of marriage brings us a partner who will help us to reach God's eternal kingdom.

Some of you may also be considering a lifelong commitment to being single. People who choose this vocation often do so because they have a specialized career that takes most of their focused time. For example, a scientist working on the cure for cancer is involved in a worthy goal that demands most of his time and attention. Other people choose a single vocation in order to better care for their aging parents.

WHAT IS DISCERNMENT?

No one is asking you to pick a vocation in one sitting! It doesn't work that way. Actually, determining your vocation is best done over time through a process called *discernment.*

Mainly, discerning your mission involves prayer. It means praying over a decision, asking for guidance of the Holy Spirit, and, finally, actually making a decision, acting on it, and evaluating it. Consider these three steps:

- *Step One: Dream and Imagine.* Take some quiet prayer time to picture yourself in a couple of different vocations. For example, you may have a love for science and medicine and imagine yourself as a researcher or even a doctor.

How would this type of a life play out as a single person? As a spouse and parent? Is there any way you might also combine your love for science with a religious vocation as a priest or religious? (You may wish to explore the life of Gregor Mendel, an Augustinian priest who was also a scientist and one of the founders of the new science of genetics in the nineteenth century.) To be able to dream and imagine several possibilities for your life is one of the great gifts of freedom that God offers you. You should also thank God that you live in a country that offers the opportunity to make free choices. Make your dreams big and open to all kinds of possibilities. At this age, don't limit yourself. Never forget the words the angel spoke to the Blessed Virgin Mary when she was told that she would be the Mother of God, even though she was not married and not been with a man: "For nothing will be impossible for God" (Lk 1:37). With God, nothing is impossible for you either.

- *Step Two: Gather Information.* Think about any big decision you have made up to this point in your life. For example, did you have a voice in choosing the high school you attend? If so, what kind of process was involved? Likely it included making a list of the strengths and weaknesses of any schools you were considering. In order to make lists of those kinds, you had to have plenty of information. What types of courses did the schools offer? Did the athletic or performing arts programs meet your interests? How far was the campus from your home, and how would you be able to get there? What social opportunities would you have? In answering these types of questions you were able to gather enough information to make a decision on where

you enrolled for high school. You have likely already be-
gun the same type of process for choosing a college. This
step of gathering information also is necessary for beginning to make a decision about a life vocation. If you have
dreamed and imagined yourself as a priest or religious,
take some time to find out about requirements for enter-
ing the seminary or novitiate. Also, look ahead and discover
what seminary life is like and what it would take for you
to be ordained. Or, explore the variety of religious com-
munities that are available. Which have missions that are
most in tune for what you want to do with your life? This
type of research can be done both formally on the Internet
and informally through conversations with priests, nuns, or
brothers. Gathering information about marriage is a little
different. You can certainly observe a variety of married
couples, young and old, and ask them about the rewards
and challenges of married life. These should be couples
that vary in age from their twenties to the age of your
grandparents. Finally, temper your dreams with a dose of
reality. No matter what Christian vocation you are considering, think about all of the obstacles that would go into this
vocation that may have to do with your education, health,
and age.

- *Step Three: Pray.* When you first begin to pray over a vocation, the focus of the prayer is on the "big picture" of the
vocation. After you have gathered information, this is the
time to center yourself with God, to gauge your feelings
with respect to both your emotions and the options you
have uncovered through your research. This should all be
done from the perspective of trying to understand what it is

God wants for your life. Call on the Holy Spirit. The more you pray and consider all of the vocational options, the more likely that God's voice will clearly merge with yours. You and the Lord will be speaking the same tune. You will eventually have a clear understanding of what God wants of you and how you can follow his will.

Discovering your vocation for life and determining God's will is no small task. But you don't have to be overly concerned about the direction of this process when you remember two things:

1. God is in control of your life.
2. He wants only the best for you.

You can take great comfort in knowing that God loves and cares so much for you that he has a special plan for your life, and he will guide you to it. As the Book of Proverbs teaches:

> Many are the plans in a man's heart, but it is the decision of the Lord that endures. (Prv 19:21)

YOUR MISSION TO LOVE

The Gospel of John (21:15–19) tells of a somewhat strange conversation between the risen Jesus and St. Peter along the shores of the Sea of Tiberias. Jesus and the disciples had just finished eating breakfast when the Lord began to question Peter: "Simon, son of John, do you love me more than these?" The original Greek translation of the Bible reveals that Jesus used the most intimate form of the word love, *agape*.

Peter responds to Jesus clearly: "Yes, Lord, you know that I love you." There was a difference in Peter's word choice for love, however. The Greek New Testament records Peter using the word *phile*, not *agape*, for love. *Phile* describes a less committed form of love. It is the type of love two friends might have for one another.

Jesus asks Peter again: "Simon, *agape*?" Peter answers the same way: "Yes, Lord, *phile*."

The conversation is not over. Jesus says: "Simon, Son of John, do you love me?" This time, Jesus has restated the question and used the same word that Peter used, *phile*. Jesus loves Peter so much that he is willing to meet the level of love and commitment that Peter can provide at this time. This is an important message for you to hear as well.

Jesus wants you to love him deeply. He wants you to make a commitment to be his disciple. He wants you to follow the Father's will. He wants you to love. He wants you to offer all that you have. He wants your whole life. He wants you to be committed to him. But, as with Peter, for now he will accept whatever level of love and commitment that you can muster.

I received an e-mail from seventeen-year-old Katie. She told me that she felt like a loser. She had started a relationship with a boy when she was in tenth grade. They were both Catholics, and they kept their space physically, not even kissing until after several months of dating.

From there, Katie said, the physical temptations grew stronger. Her boyfriend started to pressure her to have sex. One day he told her to come to his house. He said that his parents would be home. But they were not there. The boy forced himself on Katie. She wrote: "I tried to get away, and I fought with every ounce of strength I had. I prayed with all my heart and begged God to help me. I was raped that day."

Katie's anguish grew. She didn't tell anyone what had happened. She was depressed, and her grades plummeted from a 3.8 GPA to barely passing.

Life began to change for the better for Katie when she went on a retreat. She wrote, "I realized that I was being self-absorbed. What was I thinking? My parents love me. God loves me. I wasn't going to ruin my dreams and goals for life because of what happened."

When you come to a moment of faith like Katie did, be sure to look for clues to your life mission or vocation at the same time. I know that when God touched my life, I immediately wanted to begin to serve him. My life since then has been a progression of this ministry I am involved in now. God was with me every step of the way.

When Charles de Foucauld kept repeating his "strange prayer," a priest at St. Augustine's Church suggested that he make a good confession. The wheels of God's providence were set in motion at that time. Charles would eventually give up his wealth; live a life of poverty, prayer, and solitude—mostly in the desert—and later become a priest. Charles later remembered the day he went to confession at St. Augustine's: "My religious vocation dates from the same hour as my faith: God is so great."

Questions to Help You Win It All

1. What are my passions?

2. What kind of career would I like to have?

3. How can I serve God in my work?

4. What would it take for me to consider the priesthood or religious life?

5. With whom can I share the dreams of my vocation?

6. What can I learn in prayer about my life's mission?

STEPS TO DISCOVER YOUR MISSION IN LIFE

- Write your mission statement for life. Incorporate the teaching of the *Catechism of the Catholic Church:* "to know, to love, and to serve him, and so to come to paradise" (1721). Share your statement with your friends. Follow it.

- Find two or more people to pray with during the week. Make sure to communicate with them what you believe in and why. Stay true to your faith in Christ, and he will bless you abundantly.

- Once you know your mission in life, it is time to discern your vocation. Practice the three steps of discernment (pages 29–32). For the time being, what type of vocation does it reveal? Find a spiritual mentor (priest, coach, teacher) who can help you to explore your mission, vocation, and career.

Make Your Mess Your Message

THE CHALLENGES WE FACE

We all have messy lives. No one lives a life that is smooth sailing from start to finish.

Do you remember the conversation Jesus had with Peter after Jesus asked him, "Who do you say that I am?" (see Mark 8: 27–38)

Peter correctly answered Jesus: "You are the Messiah."

But then the conversation got complicated. Jesus told Peter what it meant to be the Messiah. Jesus said that he must:

- suffer greatly,
- be rejected,
- be killed.

In addition, Jesus explained, those who wished to be his disciples must be willing to do the same: "Whoever wishes to come after me must deny himself, take up his cross and follow me." Complicated. Painful. Messy.

If you look up the phrase "I never promised you a rose garden" on Google, you'll find it associated with a novel, film, and song. In any of the cases, the message is similar to what Jesus is telling us. Life on earth is *not* meant to be without problems, difficulties, and suffering. To expect otherwise is to set yourself up for a life of both disappointment and fantasy. Quoting the song lyrics: "Along with the sunshine, there's gotta be a little rain sometimes."

However, Jesus didn't stop in his prediction about the rocky road that he and his disciples would face. After suffering, being rejected, and being killed for doing his Father's will, Jesus knew he would "rise after three days."

The mess or suffering of your own life can bring a similarly positive outcome. Not only can the suffering you endure now help you to a share in Christ's cross and your ultimate resurrection to life everlasting, it can bring new life to you and to others in the present as well.

This third step of your plan to *win it all* is about making the most of the messes and travails that make up your life. Not only can you personally learn from your pain and suffering, you can help others who have faced similar situations to gain insight and to avoid depression and despair.

Initially, it's important to understand that there are different kinds of messes that throw a wrench in our days. Some are just plain trivial and aren't worth spending a moment's thought on:

- I wear gel in my hair, but sometimes my hair still gets tangled.
- I get caught in a thunderstorm without an umbrella, and I am soaked.
- I am stuck behind a school bus on my way to work and then at a traffic light that takes forever to turn to green.

These kinds of messes are really inconsequential. We should accept them as part of the day that God has made. In no way should they make us upset. But I bet things like this have bothered you or someone you know to the wrong degree. Am I correct?

UNCONTROLLABLE MESSES

In this step, I am talking only about messes that matter, messes like those that affect our lives in a negative way. Some kinds of messes are uncontrollable. Think about what a young woman named Tanna shared in front of a large group of teens at a recent conference:

> On June 28, 2008, my five-year-old brother was diagnosed with a rare stomach tumor. And it was hard for me and my family to take. Why would God let this happen? He was only five years old. What did he ever do to anyone? The first two weeks were like a whirlwind. A tumor the size of his Nerf ball was removed from his stomach. Radiation and

chemo followed. Our family was separated. My
parents had to be at the hospital almost 24/7 for
nearly a year. My brother lost all of his hair. He took
all this well, maybe because he didn't know exactly
what was happening to him. But I know that I cried
my eyes out. I didn't want him to die.

Now over a year later, my brother is officially in
remission. There were wonderful doctors and God
who got him through. Today, if you saw him, you
would probably see him running around like any
other boy his age.

Tanna's sharing of her story was an inspiration to the hundreds of teens who heard it. It was especially meaningful to one teen in attendance who had just found out that a family member had been diagnosed with cancer. She and her family were at a place in the journey that Tanna and her family were at months before. She recognized what she was feeling in what Tanna had shared about her own experience. And she definitely heard the message of hope in the resolution of the story.

Your own mess, your own suffering, can have an impact on others! You just need to be willing to share.

Sharing is also what Sr. Barbara Anne, a seventy-five-year-old Franciscan nun, decided to do from her computer at the Our Lady of Angels Convent in Mishawaka, Indiana. She had read in the day's news that a football player from Boston College, Mark Herzlich, had been diagnosed with a rare bone cancer in his left leg. Sr. Barbara Anne had survived colon cancer herself. She remembered how scared she was. "God put Mark in my heart so I would write to him," she said.

> Dear Mark,
> You are young and have so many dreams to be experienced. I've lived for three-quarters of a century and am grateful for all the blessings I've been given in my lifetime. I still have a few unrealized dreams that I want to see come to fruition. So let's fight this cancer together.

The nuns have prayed for Mark twenty-four hours a day at the Franciscan convent. On October 24, 2009, when Boston College played at Notre Dame, near where Sr. Barbara Anne lives, she finally got to meet him. "I would love to see him play football again just because I know that's one of his dreams," Sister Barbara Anne said. "I think that's what it's all about. That we keep our spirits up and we trust that something good is going to come because of all this." In the spring of 2010, Mark Herzlich returned to the football practice field at Boston College.

From these stories and others like them, we know that pain often brings perfection and satisfaction. Consider athletes who put in months and months of painful weightlifting and running in order to achieve a satisfying season. Pain and suffering—all the messes of our lives—can lead to success and fulfillment.

Don't ever forget the greatest moral evil ever committed— the passion and death of God's only Son—and the subsequent good that resulted from it. From his suffering and death, Christ was raised, and we are redeemed!

An important thing is to learn from your mess and make it your message by sharing its meaning with others. Most messes typically don't strike at us like rare and dreadful diseases.

PEOPLE CAN BE MEAN

The second kind of mess that we face is when people around us—maybe even our closest friends—do things to hurt us.

I heard from a boy named John about a friend of his since childhood. When they reached high school, the friend began to drift away. "He started using alcohol and became sexually adventurous," John shared. "When I tried to help by telling his father that I thought John was in danger, he accused me of being a liar. He told me that if I ever contacted his family again, he would physically hurt me. I have never seen John again."

Other teens have described being hurt by close friends who pit new friends or boyfriends or girlfriends against each other. One girl told how she was deeply hurt when she didn't find out for two weeks that her oldest and dearest friend had been hospitalized. "She confided in a girl who talks behind her back instead of me," she explained.

These relationship messes are perpetual; they have been going on since the beginning of time. What they most often reveal is that the person who causes the hurt of another has some deep emotional pain himself or herself. They may be depressed, or they may be jealous. Rather than feeling the sting of the pain they are sending out, we should reach out to them, forgive them, and pray for them. We should understand them.

You should also work on your own self-concept. When you begin to feel confident and good about yourself, you have a better chance of putting the hurts others try to inflict in perspective. In turn, you will be able to be more attentive to the pain of the person who strikes out against you. You can do several things to improve how you feel about yourself.

SOME WAYS TO IMPROVE YOUR SELF-CONCEPT

Are you aware of "self-talk"? This is your internal voice that is constantly relaying information, commentary, and news your way. When you sleep, this self-talk is transformed into your dreams. Sometimes this self-talk is supportive and friendly, while other times it can be negative. For example, you may be a great playground basketball player who has never tried out for a school team but would like to go for it for the next season. You may hear a voice telling you: "Don't even think about it. You wouldn't like the other players, and you would probably be cut anyway."

Negative self-talk of this kind can damage your self-concept. This is the way you see yourself and the way you believe you are seen by others. Having a healthy view of yourself is crucial for you as you navigate through the challenges and pitfalls of life. Having a healthy self-concept is also necessary for you to be able to find lessons in your messes and share what you learned with others. How can you improve your self-concept? Here are a few ways:

- Do not focus on things that are outside of your control, like negative and unproductive comments made by others. Also, while it is wise to learn from past mistakes, don't dwell on them so that they make you unproductive. Rather, reflect on what you learned from the mistakes so that you will not repeat them and so you can share the lessons you've gained with others.

- Replace negative self-talk with positive self-praise. Commend yourself when you have done well. Continue to look for ways to improve whenever possible.

- Gather a positive support group of friends and acquaintances around you. This means finding people who share not only your same interests in things like hobbies and activities, but more importantly, having friends and mentors who support your Catholic beliefs and core values.

- Again, it is important to recognize that there are some things you can control and some things you can't. Spend the majority of your time and effort working on things that you do have control over, for example, your efforts in school, your relationship with your family, your prayer life, and your service to those in need.

When you are confident and secure in who you are, you can really prosper personally and help others to learn from your experiences, both good and bad.

You may know something about the story of St. Thérèse of Lisieux. She was a young girl who entered the Carmelite convent in the nineteenth century and who symbolized herself as a "little flower." Her purpose in thinking of herself that way was to explain that like a tiny, wild flower in the forest, she survived and indeed flourished through the warmth of spring and summer as well as through the winds and snows of fall and winter. It is a good model for you to use for your life as well: Draw on both positive experiences and negative experiences. Don't let your mess bring you down!

St. Thérèse of Lisieux also practiced the ancient Church tradition of "offering it up"—that is, offering up her daily sufferings and stress for the good of others, including the souls of purgatory. When she was first in the convent, she was assigned to help an older nun walk around the corridor halls of the convent. The older sister complained all of the time: "You move too fast. I was right when I said you were too young to help me. You are going to cause me to fall." Thérèse took in the complaints, smiled, and said a prayer to "offer it up." She described this as her "little way" of taking even the smallest inconveniences of life and offering them up for a good cause.

You can only react to sufferings big and small in your life when you are grounded in a healthy self-concept that is also in touch with the Paschal Mystery—the passion, death, and resurrection—of Jesus Christ. When you pattern your life on the Paschal Mystery, everything takes on new meaning. And your peers will be able to learn from your example. You can truly make your mess your message!

A THIRD KIND OF MESS

The third kind of mess is of our own making—with the assistance of an evil force called Satan. The third kind of mess that we all experience is *sin*.

Sin is a subject that many people want to avoid. Sin is defined as an offense against God through a violation of truth, reason, and conscience. Sins are not mistakes. Our personal sins are not things that are "done to us" by another. You can't sin by accident.

St. Paul gave names for different kinds of sins in the First Letter to the Corinthians— fornication (this means sex outside of marriage), licentiousness, strife, jealousy, anger, selfishness, dissension, factions, envy, drunkenness, carousing—that contrast with the fruit of the Spirit described in Galatians 5:19–21.

If you were baptized, your sins were washed away. Your soul was cleansed. Yet sin persists. St. Paul also wrote: "How can we who died to sin yet live in it?" (Rom 6:2). You need to take stock of your life and examine your sins and avoid sinful behavior in the future.

However, we are human! Sin is unfortunately part of our nature. We are hounded by a tempter, Satan, who can even twist goodness to sinful actions. When you do sin, you must seek forgiveness and reconciliation. You must do penance. You must ask for compassion from those you offend and from God. You must be converted.

Conversion is a central message of Jesus' preaching: "Repent and believe in the Gospel" (Mk 1:14). Conversion is illustrated in Jesus' parable of the prodigal son (see Luke 15:11–32). You know the story, I'm sure. When the younger son who had abandoned his family and wasted his inheritance longed to return home and to the life he had left, he began the process of conversion. He said to himself (a form of self-talk!):

> I shall get up and go to my father and I shall say to
> him, "Father, I have sinned against you. I no longer

deserve to be called your son; treat me as you would treat one of your hired workers.

We can control the mess of our sinfulness by first loathing the sins themselves. I shared with you the story of my destructive behavior—remember when I lit myself on fire. The process of my conversion began when I finally loathed, hated, and despised what I was doing in the same way that the prodigal son hated having his meals in a pigsty.

Conversion also involves comparing our lives to the life of Jesus. Ask yourself if your life is directed toward complete union with God in the same way that Jesus' life was. If your life is really devoted to some other goal, you need to think of the implications. Are you willing to risk losing your faith, your ability to love, and your chance for Heaven for these other goals? If so, what are these goals? Money? Fame? Power? Prestige? Are these things that will truly bring you peace and contentment in this life? Will they further you along the path to a life in eternity with your family, friends, and God?

Please think about these issues. They are so important.

Catholics have a great "second chance" sacrament. It is the sacrament of Penance or Reconciliation. It is one of my favorites, and it is so important. Any time you commit a serious sin (see a list of serious sins on pages 123–125), you should go to confession. You should make it a habit to celebrate this sacrament regularly at other times of the year as well. I try to go to confession at least once a month. Do you need a reminder? How about picking the first Saturday of each month? Confession is a key to growth. It is a sacrament full of grace.

Use the sacrament to take in God's grace of forgiveness in this very particular way, a gift from Jesus.

When you use this sacrament, remember that the penitent (the person confessing) has three parts: contrition (sorrow), confession, and satisfaction (penance). The fourth part is the confessor's (the priests's) absolution (the taking away of sin).

The satisfaction or penance part of the sacrament is especially important. Usually, the priest will ask you to say some prayers to help repair some of the hurt caused by your sins. But he may ask you to do some more. This is where you can *really* turn your mess into a message.

A repentant sinner is a powerful witness to goodness.

A girl at one of the recent conferences I attended told about how she and her sister had been hurt very badly by the dance instructor at a school they had both attended for thirteen years. The teacher had violated their confidence and embarrassed them in front of the other girls in the class. The teacher said some untrue and unkind things. Both sisters ended up quitting the class—and who can blame them?

But to really make this mess their message, I called on this girl to do something more: Go back to the teacher. Thank her for her years of teaching. Affirm her. Repair the relationship.

You can do it, too. Don't lament the pain and suffering in your life. It is *part* of life, after all. Turn your mess into a positive experience. Help others to learn from your experiences and to avoid your sins. You will be helping them and yourself on the way to winning it all!

Win it All

Questions to Help You Win It All

1. Name an example of a mess in your life that was "uncontrollable."

2. When did a friend or peer hurt you? What did you do about that mess?

3. What do you believe about sin?

4. Why do you need to change?

5. How do you seek conversion?

STEPS TO MAKE YOUR MESS YOUR MESSAGE

- Repent and believe in the good news! Write a letter about the messes in your life and the growth you have experienced because of them. Give your letter to someone who might be encouraged by the lessons you have learned.

- Seek forgiveness from someone you have caused pain. Say: "I am sorry." Take her out for lunch. Spend time with him. Admit your sin or mistake. Share your heart with her.

- Commit to going to confession once per month. Examine your conscience daily. Think about times you have sinned. Celebrate the sacrament of Penance, and rejoice in its graces.

Four⁴

Keep Your Passion

LIVING LIFE TO THE FULLEST

Baseball legend Yogi Berra, known for his offbeat so-called "Yogisms" like "it's never over until it's over" and "it fees like déjà vu all over again," recently shared a bit of parting advice in a speech to college graduates. He told them to anticipate each new day as if they were like children looking forward to a birthday part, or in baseball terms, "I say go out and live your life like every day is opening day."

A close friend of mine, David Tyree, made the greatest catch in Super Bowl history while playing for the New York

Win ^{it} All

Giants. Eighteen months after the Super Bowl, David was released by the Giants. The front page of the newspaper screamed: "David Tyree; Hero to Zero." If David's only passion had been for gaining headlines and playing football, he may have been beaten by these events. But David's true passion is to live his life in service of others. He is an excellent husband and father. He wasn't defeated by his football setback at all.

Both of these athletes have a passion for living—to be able to wake up every day with the enthusiasm, commitment, desire, service, and love to live the day to its fullest. Isn't that what it's all about? Yogi Berra and David Tyree are true examples of Christian virtue.

In the second step, Discover Your Mission in Life, part of the task was to uncover your passions—what you are good at and what you like to do—and let them explode into a lifestyle or career and vocation. In this step, I want to share some more about passions, but I want to focus the discussion around three areas:

- Commitment
- Service
- Eternity

Don't forget the initial step for discovering your passion. Determining what you are good at and what you like to do is the place to get started. But those are only starting points. The first wave of emotion will take you only so far. Isn't this what happened with Peter and his brother Andrew? If you remember, they were a bit impetuous when Jesus passed by as they were casting their nets into the Sea of Galilee. Jesus said to them, "Come after me, and I will make you fishers of men" (Mk 1:17).

This was an unusual request! "Fishers of men"? What could that mean? More importantly, how would Peter and Andrew know what it meant? In any case, their eagerness got the best of them. They left their fishing nets and followed Jesus.

A little further along the shore, James, the son of Zebedee, and his brother John were even more zealous. When Jesus called them, they left all of their employees and their father in the boat and followed him!

It's not unusual to have that much passion for something— at least at the very start. Have you ever been the person who:

- got all jazzed about something—let's say music—and had your parents purchase a musical instrument and sign you up for lessons, only to see your practice time wane by the week, until just a short time later the instrument was stuffed in the back of a closet?

- promised yourself that "this would be the semester" that you would raise your grade point average, only to give up when you realized that doing well in your most difficult courses actually involved putting in more than the assigned time for study?

- decided that even though some of your family doesn't go regularly to Mass any longer that you would, until the weather turned from fall to winter and the warm blankets on the cold Sunday morning felt better than getting out of bed "on my only day to sleep in"?

A commitment to winning it all is worth it! Keeping commitments *can* be hard, including your commitment to be a disciple of Jesus Christ. Ask Peter, Andrew, James, and John: see the Garden of Gethsemane. Jesus knows this. He told a parable comparing those who keep commitments to those who don't.

BEARING FRUIT THROUGH PERSEVERANCE

The parable Jesus told about keeping commitments is about a sower, or farmer, who goes out to plant some seed:

> And as he sowed, some seed fell on the path and was trampled, and the birds of the sky ate it up. Some seed fell on rocky ground, and when it grew, it withered for lack of moisture. Some seed fell among thorns, and the thorns grew with it and choked it. And some seed fell on good soil, and when it grew, it produced fruit a hundredfold." (Lk 8:5–8)

One of the things the parable is really teaching about is that there are some obstacles in your life that can keep you from keeping your commitments, especially in living the kind of Christian life you know that you want to live. For one, there are outside forces in your life—represented by the birds—who try to snatch away your beliefs. Think about someone—maybe you—who has made the commitment to quit drinking or smoking, or to begin a healthier diet, only to have peers bring the temptations of a party, a cigarette to smoke, or a donut to eat. Other "birds" are present that may make you doubt your Catholic faith: unseemly movies or music lyrics, friends who belittle religion, and even teachers in school who may be agnostic or atheists.

While there are outside forces that keep you from your commitments, there may also be factors within your own life that can contribute to times that you give up. People—today especially—come predisposed with a "rocky" attitude that leaves them with a distracted attention span and ready to move on to a new interest at a moment's notice. Just think of the tabloid or sound byte media culture where the public is always ready to focus on one sensational story for a day or two before moving on to the next. Your commitment to faith cannot be like that! Don't let boredom or laziness get in the way of your promise to follow Jesus. And don't let an illness, painful death, broken relationship, or even serious sin keep you from seeking out God's love.

Also, the parable mentions "thorns" as things in our life that can crowd out what's important, especially something most important, like God. You can list several things, such as school, friendships, sports, popularity, and television, that can keep you from Christ. Take some time to sift through these thorns in order to keep your commitment to faith.

Don't forget: To be passionate about anything—relationships, career, vocation, or your faith mission—demands a solid commitment. Expend some effort to overcome the obstacles that keep you from following through.

Think about it like this: I once told the students in my class that there were plenty of their classmates who were passionate. These classmates were passionate about getting trashed every Friday night. Others were passionate with all their hearts about smoking weed. A boy stopped me and asked why I was describing people like that as passionate. He said that was "stupid." I said, "No, what is stupid is when others are more passionate about those harmful and destructive things than we are to the life God asks of us."

MAKING A DIFFERENCE

Our passions are only personal unless we use them to make a difference in the lives of others. This means making sure that no matter what our mission or vocation is in life, whatever we are good at and like to do, that we add a component of service.

In order to serve well, you must first come to realize that the first and best gift you have really has nothing to do with what you like and what you are good at. Your first gift is that you were made in the image of a good and loving Creator God. This alone is enough to make you valuable and to take your self-concept off the charts. Yet, in addition to this most valuable gift, you were blessed with other talents and abilities. These are not meant to compensate for anything you feel is lacking in your life, but rather are to be celebrated because they add to your already unique and good self.

St. Paul wrote that "there are different kinds of spiritual gifts but the same Spirit; there are different forms of service but the same Lord" (1 Cor 12:4–5). The message is that there is nothing better or worse about being either an athlete or the smartest student in the school. You are called to develop your personal passions, not only to make *you* better, but to be able to share your passions with others.

How do you serve? To put it simply: using your passions to serve others involves looking at the people you meet, especially the most needy, as "other selves." What do they need? How can you bring your gifts—as simple or as elaborate as they might be—to their aid?

You may be shocked by how much you have to offer. In 2009, Pope Benedict XVI canonized one of the newest saints, St. Damien De Veuster. Born in Belgium, Damien thought he would be a farmer like his other relatives. He was called to be a priest. However, the superiors at the seminary did not want him at first because they didn't think he was smart enough. They finally relented, and he was allowed to begin his studies for the priesthood. Damien prayed constantly to the patron saint of missionaries, St. Francis Xavier, for the chance to follow in his footsteps. Just prior to his ordination, Damien was allowed to move to Hawaii as a missionary.

On the island of Molokai was a leper colony. Fr. Damien wrote, "I can only attribute to God an undeniable feeling that soon I shall join them." Six months after he arrived in Molokai, he wrote, "I make myself a leper with the lepers to gain all for Jesus Christ." St. Damien would never leave the lepers. After he contracted leprosy, he was relieved, for he thought it made him more like them.

Think about the development of his vocation: from the desire to be a priest, to the desire to travel thousands of miles from his home to a mission, to the desire, ultimately, to take on the dreadful illness of those he served.

Project your own passion out to the vast space of the future. Where will it take you? Think big and bold and dramatic.

How can you use what may seem like simple gifts from simple circumstances to serve others? Could you possibly become a saint like Damien De Veuster?

Why not?

A PASSION FOR HEAVEN

Life is short. A good friend of mine who is seventy years old once told me, "Life is like a roll of toilet paper. In the beginning it seems like you have a lot. When you get to the end it goes quick."

Have you ever known someone your age—a teenager—who has died? I have met or heard of a few teens who have recently died.

One was a very good baseball player named Brad. He was finishing up his senior season at a high school in California and had already been recruited to play ball the next year for a junior college team. Striding to the plate to take his turn at bat, Brad winked at his parents and his girlfriend, and coolly splattered a bubble from the two wads of gum he always kept in his mouth. It was the third pitch that hit Brad squarely in the center of his chest. The gum was caught in his windpipe. One of those freaky things that happen. Brad died before the paramedics even arrived.

Sophia was another young woman I knew. She was at the top of her high school class in academics. Her mom remembered worrying about her when she lived at home because she was such a homebody and didn't seem to do much socially. When Sophia left for her freshman year of college, her mom encouraged her to be more outgoing and to broaden her experience beyond only studying. At a dorm party just about six weeks after staring school, Sophia unknowingly took a drink that had been spiked with a drug that when combined with a cold medication she was taking caused her to pass out. She was in a coma for four weeks before she died a few days before Thanksgiving.

Check the news or the obituaries. There are people your age reported on the daily news channels who have been killed in car accidents or have passed away after brave fights trying to ward off cancer or other nasty and virulent diseases. Men and women just a few years older than you are—both Americans and from other nations—are being killed in war.

Please pause and share a prayer for these people whom I have described and remember them to Jesus, Mary, Joseph, the saints, and the angels. I bring up these miserable, sad stories for one reason: to remind you of the fragile nature of human life. The reality of existence is that we never really know when we wake up in the morning whether the day is our last. Speaking of the end of the world, but also applicable to our own deaths, Jesus said, "But of that day and hour no one knows, neither the angels of heaven, nor the Son, but the Father alone" (Mt 24:36).

We should prepare for our deaths by living with a sense of urgency that we are only given a certain amount of time on earth. (I will discuss more about this in Step 8: Live Every Day as If It Were Your Last.) Realizing this, isn't it common sense to understand that the vast majority of the infinite time that we will live will be spent somewhere else? Blessed Junipero Serra, a Franciscan priest who founded many of the California missions, once said, "Life is uncertain and, in fact, may be very brief. If we compare it with eternity, we will clearly realize that it cannot be but more than an instant."

It is through this awareness that your life is fragile and uncertain that you should develop a passion for what comes next—Heaven. This passion first of all involves a clear understanding and a follow-through of how to get there!

As Catholics, we know that at death all people receive rewards for their lives. Those who have committed to Christ wholeheartedly and live a good life merit eternal reward because of his great love for us, and those who have died while separated from God receive their chosen punishment. This means that you will spend eternal life in either Heaven or Hell. Heaven is eternal life spent with God and everyone who shares in God's life. Hell is eternal separation from God. To win it all, we choose Heaven with all of our heart.

Heaven is the place where time will have no control over us. It is a place where we will be reunited with our family members and friends who have died before us. It is a place where we will never experience sickness, disease, pain, and suffering again. The great Christian writer C. S. Lewis described some more of the differences between Heaven and Hell:

> In Hell they talk a lot about love.
> In Heaven they just do it.
>
> Hell is an unending church service without God.
> Heaven is God without a church service.

In Hell everything is pornographic and no one is excited.
In Heaven everything is exciting and there is no pornography.

In Hell there is sex without pleasure.
In Heaven there is pleasure without sex.

Hell is a bad dream from which you never wake up.
Heaven is waking from which you never need to sleep.

As cool as this description is of Heaven, even it cannot begin to encompass what Heaven will really be like. St. Paul wrote, "What eye has not seen, and ear has not heard, and what has not entered the human heart, what God has prepared for those who love him" (1 Cor 2:9). You can't have a greater passion in this life than doing *everything* it takes to assure that you reach Heaven. St. Vincent Pallotti once advised:

Remember that the Christian life is one of action; not of speech and daydreams. I intend that every moment of time past, present, and future be used by me and all creatures in the best way. In Heaven we shall rest.

You are free to choose! Choose well! Make it your number-one goal to get to Heaven. When you use your gift of freedom in the right way to choose goodness over evil and model your life on the Savior, Jesus Christ, he promises that Heaven is ours! Conversely, when we choose self over God, we become heartless. God respects our freedom and will give us what we want for eternity.

Win the whole thing! Win it all! Heaven awaits!

CHOOSE A SIDE:
A LITTLE MORE ABOUT PASSION!

The thing about passion is that you have to choose a side.

Don't be all about Heaven if you are not ready to make sacrifices.

Don't waffle from one side to the other.

Don't say "whatever."

Don't go halfway. Give it all you've got.

Don't forget the words from Revelation 3:16: "So, because you are lukewarm, neither hot nor cold, I will spit you out of my mouth."

Are you in or out?

I am going to make a strange comparison here.

Do you know the rapper called 50 Cent? Do you know the holy nun named Mother Teresa?

They both have something in common. What?!

Yes, it's true. Curtis Jackson III said he picked the name "50 Cent" as a "metaphor for change." As a young boy, after his mother died, he lived with his grandmother and openly sold drugs. When he was arrested going through a metal detector at school, he said he was "embarrassed that I got arrested like that."

50 Cent has been shot. He has been sued (by his ex-girlfriend). He has written several controversial songs. He is rich.

It is not all good stuff about Curtis Jackson III, from his difficult childhood to some bad choices he has made as an adult. But another thing is true about him: he is what he is. He does not do anything halfway. While his passions have not always been directed to positive outcomes, at least he does have passion! I appreciated his passion so much that in 2004 I decided to ask more than five hundred young people to write letters to 50 Cent to encourage him to change. Did it happen? Who knows? Could it happen? Absolutely.

Pray for 50 Cent. He is a father. He also has passion about raising his son!

Mother Teresa was not a rapper! But what she has in common with 50 Cent is that she didn't live her life halfway either. You might say that Mother Teresa, for the most part, lived out on the other edge of life from 50 Cent.

Her passion led to life-altering decisions.

One of the first of these was when she arrived in India in 1929. She took her final vows as a nun and began to teach in eastern Calcutta. She was distressed by the poverty she saw each day in the streets that encroached right up to the school. Mother Teresa prayed for these people until one day she heard God tell her to help them herself. She left her religious community in 1948 to form the Missionaries of Charity.

She explained, "God still loves the world, and he sends you and me to be his love and compassion to the poor."

Make a choice. Which side will you be on? Pick one. Don't play it down the middle. Give life everything you've got. Winning it all is about making the choices and living the life today that can guarantee you Heaven. 50 Cent or Mother Teresa?

Win it All

I am going with Mother Teresa! And I don't want to be anywhere in between.

Questions to Help You Win It All

1. What is something you once had great passion for that has now waned? Why did it wane?

2. What keeps you from making a full commitment to Jesus Christ?

3. How do you think of Heaven?

4. Tell how you are not lukewarm in your faith.

5. How will you get to Heaven?

STEPS TO KEEP YOUR PASSION

- "Just begin, one, one, one," Mother Teresa said. "Begin at home by saying something good to someone in your family. Begin by helping someone in need in your community, at work, or at school. Begin by making whatever you do something beautiful for God." Begin today.

- Be passionate about your life story. Be passionate about who you are. Go to www.justinfatica.net and write your story on the Win It All Wall of Hope.

- Commit to eliminating one sin that is really hurting you and others. Commit to change and be passionate about changing no matter the cost.

Five⁵

Remain Fearless

HEALTH AND UNHEALTHY FEARS

The title of this fifth step hints at something that is impossible in many ways. Remain fearless? You already know that fear is a natural and necessary emotion.

There surely are many healthy fears. Toddlers seem to have no fear. But imagine if that were really true. Parents would be driven even crazier with worry that their young child might leap from the top of the stairs or put a little hand in a fire. Fear is an emotion that offers natural protection from danger. This is true at your age as well. Fear may a big reason you refrain from driving your car too fast or staying out past curfew. Maybe it is only the fear of your parents' punishment that keeps you from dangerous situations, but it is fear nonetheless!

What I mean by remaining fearless is the elimination of *unhealthy fears.*

There are some normal fears that you face in day-to-day situations that can be lessened, if not eliminated altogether. For example, you may fear giving an oral presentation in class or answering aloud any time a teacher calls on you. You may seem paralyzed with fear before a final exam even though in reality you know the material backward and forward. With taking steps to improve your self-concept (see Step 3), you will grow in confidence so that all but the most necessary tensions and nervousness can disappear and you can share more of your true self in any situation.

Some other fears are more severe and less healthy. You may be afraid that no one likes you, even your closest friends. This may lead you to fear that you are completely alone. This is known as the fear of abandonment.

You may be afraid for someone you care about, like your mother or father or one of your siblings. Maybe you are afraid that your parents' arguing with one another will escalate to the point that they will split up. Or, if they are already divorced, you may fear that their relationship will deteriorate even further to where it continues to affect your life.

You may have a heightened fear of yourself or your parents or siblings becoming dreadfully ill. This fear may be unfounded, or it could be based on your family's history of heart disease or alcoholism. You may be afraid that a brother or sister or a really close friend is messed up with alcohol or drugs, involved in a sexual relationship, or caught up with abusive companions.

There are fears of other dangerous situations that involve you. You may be fearful that you will give in to the pressures associated with sexuality, drinking, partying, vandalizing, or other situations that may be rampant among your classmates and friends. If any of these are your fears, you need to look for Jesus in these difficult situations. The risen Jesus said to Mary Magdalene and the other Mary on the way to Galilee, "Do not be afraid" (Mt 28:10).

Jesus comes to you to calm your fears. You can call on him for strength. You can call on Jesus and the Holy Spirit to be with you as you face the pressures of growing from your teenage years to adulthood. You can also practice several techniques for avoiding negative peer pressure. When you master some techniques like those described below, you will be able to eliminate or reduce a large number of unhealthy fears.

DEALING WITH PRESSURES

Negative peer pressure is a huge challenge to people of any age, but especially teenagers. It occurs when you are with people who are trying to persuade you to do something that you don't want to do or that is against what you and your family value. It often does involve making potentially harmful decisions that can lead to the occasion of sin.

How can you avoid negative peer pressure? A few different strategies can help. For example:

- *Avoid people and situations that could cause trouble.* If you know that there is going to be drugs or alcohol at a party, or it is going to be a hook-up event, avoid the party. If you know someone who has been abusive to women in the past, think two or three times before you start up a relationship with him. Now, here's an important caveat: your peers who are making dangerous and sinful choices need your positive Christian influence. In your growing self-confidence and self-esteem, look for ways that you can share your example with them so that they are not abandoned to a life that could spiral downward even further. Look for opportunities to share your friendship, support, and love. Begin by praying for them and their well-being as soon as you can. Now!

- *Know how to say "no."* You don't need to explain yourself. Well, in fact, you may be asked to explain why you don't want to do something that goes against what you believe and value, but you really don't need to. If a person tries to persuade you to do the opposite of what you want, change the subject. If that doesn't work, get away. There may be another less risky time when you can explain your decision to the person, but when there is immediate risk present, this is not the time.

- *"Put on Jesus Christ."* St. Paul said that we should "conduct ourselves properly as in the day, not in orgies and drunkenness, not in promiscuity and licentiousness, not in rivalry and jealousy" and that we should "put on the Lord Jesus Christ and make no provision for the desires of the flesh" (Rom 13:13–14). In Baptism, you become one with Christ. But it's up to you through instruction, prayer, and the practice of your faith to make sure that Jesus is at the tip of your tongue and in the natural reflexes of your actions.

When you hear about peer pressure, it is mostly in the context of *negative* peer pressure. But don't forget you have likely been encouraged, inspired, and "pressured" by friends and classmates to do many positive things as well. When you see others working hard to fit in and do well academically or through participating on a team or in a performing arts event, their examples may have touched a vein in you to do well, too.

Don't forget that the element of positive peer pressure can also have an effect on those who are trying to negatively influence you the other way. Your light will overcome their darkness.

I know this in many different ways and through many different things that have happened to me. One of the times when I should have been very afraid, I wasn't. I like to think that what kept the situation from ending up badly was faith and love.

Here's what happened: Along with some other adult leaders, I took some teens to a big event called Soulfest. A couple of the boys did something wrong when they were there. We found out that they were stealing, and we sent them back to their rooms. This was a big punishment because all of the others got to hang out in what was a really great arcade.

The next thing I knew one of the boys we sent up to the room was heading toward the lobby. "Where are you going?" I demanded. "You need to be in your room."

This boy—his name was Isaiah—told me to move aside. He said, "I'm going to kill you." Then, to prove it, he pulled out a knife and put the point right up against my neck.

I can tell you my honest words and reaction. I screamed at Isaiah, "Kill me right now. But even if you do, I will still love you."

The cops arrived, and there seemed to be about 150 people gathered around us. The knife was still lodged against my neck. "I can't take away the pain you've had in your life," I said.

He started crying. "You don't know my life."

And it was true. My heart was pounding, but I had to stand strong and tall for what was right. I knew about some of the pain that Isaiah went through but I didn't know all of his pain. I didn't know every part of his life. He and the other boys needed to know that I cared that deeply for them. What better way than to love them when one of them had a knife to my neck? That is what Jesus would have done.

Isaiah pulled the knife back and collapsed in tears.

I know it's not easy being your age. God knows this, too. But as the prophet Isaiah says:

> They that hope in the Lord will renew their strength,
>> they will soar as with eagles' wings;
> They will run and not grow weary,
>> walk and not grow faint. (Is 41:30)

God is with you as you work to conquer the very real fears of your day and age and the pressures that come from people and situations around you. God understands how difficult it is for you to grow up in the world today. Tell the Lord about your fears. He is with you. Things are not so scary when you share them with the Holy One—Father, Son, and Holy Spirit.

These types of pressures do not need to make you afraid. The Lord is always near!

OVERCOMING IRRATIONAL FEARS

Fear is one of the strongest human emotions or passions. Fear, like the other passions, can work for good or evil, "taken up into the *virtues* or perverted by the *vices*" *(Catechism of the Catholic Church,* 1768).

Having irrational fears is really an offense against your God-given freedom. Irrational fear can paralyze you and prevent you from reaching your full potential.

Sometimes this happens around the time after high school graduation. Surely some people have good reasons for not going away to college. Expenses or other situations at home may prevent it. But typically, there are some qualified students who don't want to leave their homes to go away and live at college because they are afraid. Who knows how they might have been challenged and grown if they had given this type of independence a chance?

Other times, fear can squelch a potential religious vocation. Usually, this isn't the fear of the young man who feels called to the priesthood or to a young woman who is attracted to the consecrated life of a sister. Mostly, it is the fears of their parents. In other times, Catholic parents had larger families, and it was a common practice for mothers and fathers to encourage one or more of their children to be a priest or a sister. Nowadays it is different. Parents fear that their children might "miss out" on something in their lives or "not be content" if they accept God's calling and choose one of these vocations.

Win ^{it} All

The Diocese of Des Moines, Iowa, recently cited a study of its own priests that disputes and squashes these fears. For example, parents worry:

- "I want my son to be fulfilled." Ninety-eight percent of our priests describe priesthood as life-giving.
- "I don't want my son to be lonely." Ninety-one percent of our priests report close friendships. Ninety-six percent say relationships with married couples is vital.
- "I want my son to like his work." One hundred percent of our priests say presiding at Eucharist is a great privilege. Ninety-eight percent love to preach. One hundred percent find tending to the sick to be a profound experience.
- "I want my son to be a man of prayer." Ninety-one percent of our priests say praying over the scriptures each day is important.
- "I don't want my son to regret his decision." Ninety-four percent of our priests say they would recommend priesthood to a young man. Ninety-three percent say they want to help foster vocations.

What are some irrational fears that you have? Do you think you are not "good enough" to succeed? Do you ever feel unloved? Do you feel completely solitary or alone in the world? Do ever feel so worthless that you imagine that even God couldn't possibly love you?

Irrational fears of any kind limit our God-given freedom. The good news is that you are free to change! You can fight back against irrational fears, primarily by cooperating with Christ's grace, his friendship, and the gifts of the Holy Spirit. With prayer and acts of self-denial, you can gain the confidence to cooperate with God's will so that you can fulfill your true potential as a disciple of Jesus Christ!

TWO CHRISTIANS WHO OVERCAME FEAR

I had a knife pressed against my neck. I have to admit I was a little bit afraid. But I could feel the presence of God with me during that entire situation. And I didn't want what could have been my last act on earth to be one of denial. The Church is filled with stories of *martyrs* who overcame their fears to make the ultimate sacrifice for the Lord—their own lives. Stories of two Christian martyrs—one from many, many years ago and the other from during World War II—have inspired me to consider the possibilities of living with total confidence in the Lord. I pray that I can be so strong! I pray that Christ will inspire you to live without fear!

St. Blandine died for her faith in 177 in Lyons, France. This was an era in the Roman Empire when Christianity was illegal. She was a young slave girl who was to be tortured with others. Her captors worried that she was so frail that she would immediately wilt under the cruelty they would dish out in the public amphitheatre. Blandine turned out to be the strongest of the group. She was taken down from the stake and returned to prison because none of the animals would attack her. Only on the last day of the tortures, after scourgings, after being burned alive, was she impaled and killed by a wild bull. Her only words were, "I am a Christian."

You may know the story of St. Maximilian Kolbe. He was a Catholic priest imprisoned by the Nazis at Auschwitz. On July 30, 1941, when the Nazis discovered that one of the prisoners had escaped, they were determined to enact vengeance by randomly executing ten other prisoners. One of the unlucky prisoners chosen was a Jew, Sgt. Francis Gajowniczek, who cried out in tears, "My poor wife and children! I will never see them again!"

Maximilian motioned the Nazi commander over and whispered to him, "I would like to take the place of Sgt. Gajowniczek." The commander didn't care. He just needed ten men to execute. Kolbe was pushed into the starvation bunker. He survived until August 14, when the Nazi guards came in and gave him and four other men a lethal injection. Maximilian did give a reason for why he chose to die in another man's place. He said simply, "I am a Catholic priest."

Martyrdom is *supreme witness* to the truth of the gospel. Would you have the courage to give up your life if called on in the name of Jesus Christ? Would I?

I don't know the answer to those questions, but I do know that all of us are called to take part in the life of the Church and to witness to the gospel by both words and, more importantly, actions. You know the pain that is sometimes involved in proclaiming your faith. You can be teased by all and shunned by your friends. This is an occasion to truly remain fearless! Know that Jesus is with you, supporting you in this brave effort. Don't give up!

THE RIGHT KIND OF FEAR

One of the seven gifts of the Holy Spirit that are conferred on you in the sacrament of Confirmation is the "fear of the

Lord." What could this mean? Does it mean that you should be afraid of God?

No. In fact, of all the healthy fears that you should possess, "fear of the Lord" is the most natural. The Book of Proverbs says that "fear of the Lord is the beginning of knowledge; wisdom and instruction fools despise." This gift can also be thought of as wonder and awe at being in God's presence.

When you fear the Lord, you have a clear understanding of who God is and who you are not. God is Creator. You are his creation. The amazing thing about this is that you were not created to be a servant of a vengeful, power-hungry ruler. Rather, in his love and compassion, the Father created you to be a brother or sister in the Lord. Jesus said, "You are my friends if you do what I command you" (Jn 15:14).

This great gift of God allows you to be awed and wowed by the world around you and to embrace all of its challenges, rather than to run and cower in fear. It encourages you to step up and be bold in your faith, to not give in to what could be deadly pressures of your peers, and to not be incapacitated by an internal voice that tells you what you can't do. Rather, hear God calling you to all the great possibilities life has for you.

This healthy "fear of the Lord" also reminds you that in spite of God seeming so large and beyond you, he comes to you as a small child born in a cave. This gift reminds you also that God loves and cares for you even more than you could ever love and care for yourself.

Questions to Help You Win It All

1. What are healthy fears?

2. What is one of your unhealthy fears?

3. How can you overcome unhealthy fears?

4. Who is someone who has inspired you with a dramatic witness of his or her faith?

5. What does it mean to you to be in awe of God's presence?

STEPS TO REMAIN FEARLESS

- Write five fears you might have about considering a vocation to the priesthood or religious life. Talk over these fears with a priest, sister, or brother whom you know and trust.

- Go to a sporting event and root for the visiting team. Be vocal but not rude. Get booed and dissed and see how you react. In the coming weeks, stand up for a person who gets picked on, regardless of how people treat you for doing so. Remember the game you went to as an inspiration.

- Who is someone who intimidates you? Speak to that person, discussing his or her gifts and talents and why he or she is special.

Commit
to Loving

LOVE IS THE ANSWER

To "win it all" you need to love. Love is the perfect emotion. In the end, love trumps any other passion or feeling we might have. Love leads us to do things we could have never imagined. Love really is the answer. Love will be able to do the impossible!

Jesus knew this to be so. The Lord was used to speaking in parables and to revealing his mission and identity in small bites, not in one large dose. His intention was to draw people to him in faith and to allow them the opportunity to freely accept or reject him.

Win it All

But this "plan" seemed to be put on hold when Jesus got word that his friend Lazarus, the brother of two other close friends, Martha and Mary, was ill at his home in Bethany, a small village just outside of Jerusalem in Judea (see John 11:1–44). The news got Jesus' attention because he "loved Martha and her sister and Lazarus."

Jesus had just been in Judea, and some of his enemies had tried to stone him there. Nevertheless, after waiting for two days, Jesus decided to return to attend to Lazarus because, in fact, Jesus tells them that "Lazarus has died." His disciples, remembering what had happened before, did not want to go back there. Thomas, who later doubted Jesus, said (we can imagine sarcastically), "Let us also go to die with him."

Martha greeted Jesus' arrival and seemed perturbed: "Lord, if you had been here, my brother would not have died." She expressed confidence that Jesus could still help Lazarus. Mary said the same thing to Jesus, moving him to tears. Some of the observers noticed this and said, "See how he loved him."

Jesus called in prayer to the Father so that everyone could hear. When Lazarus was raised, it was the occasion of Jesus' most dramatic and greatest miracle in the Gospels, the raising of a dead man to new life. This was not a parable or veiled message. The example was there for all to witness.

The message of this great miracle is that Jesus loves his friends. He will do anything for them. We are his friends, too. Jesus will do anything for us because of the great love he has for us.

HOW TO LOVE

At Baptism, you receive the virtue of love, which first and foremost enables you to love God. God has loved you first. The First Commandment requires you to return that love to God and to love him above everything else—in heart, soul, and mind.

Do you also remember the Great Commandment? In it, Jesus equated love for God with love for others:

> You shall love the Lord, your God, with all your heart, with all your soul, and with all your mind. This is the greatest and first commandment. The second is like it: "You shall love your neighbor as yourself." (Mt 22:37–39)

You experience love in the variety of relationships you share. You love your parents, siblings, grandparents, and friends in different ways. You also have a common love for all people and all of creation, including animals. Jesus also demands that you love your enemies. In loving in all of these ways, you are able to love God.

But hold on! Love isn't always so easy. One of the first requirements of being able to love others is to be able to love yourself.

Healthy self-love is opposite from narcissism, the kind of mentality that has people always checking their appearance or bragging about their abilities or promoting things they can do. Healthy self-love is observable in people who are comfortable with themselves and confident in most situations. Their lives are dedicated to living for the sake of others.

I was reminded of this type of person when I received a letter from a teenager who had heard me speak at a large rally. He wrote about the pain he experienced after a friend of his committed suicide. He also wrote how his parents, with six children living at home, were experiencing severe money problems. His letter ended with, "I am not a quitter."

In fact, for some reason, this boy's persistence translated into working as hard as he could to get me to come speak to his parish in his small town of Westphalia, Michigan. He said he wanted his parents to hear the same message—"how to win it all"—that he had heard at the rally. How could I say no? This young man was so committed to his parents, siblings, and friends that he wanted to bring them a message of hope. This was true love that could be witnessed only because of his outward self-confidence and self-love. Because of his efforts I did go and spend time with him at his parish. I pray that his family and all of the people whom I met in Westfalia, Michigan, are continually uplifted by him and the message of hope, love, and truth of the gospel.

When you have a healthy love for yourself, you will want to share it. Love can't remain by itself. You already know this to be true, I'm sure.

UNCONDITIONALLY LOVING

Mother Teresa shared a story about a child of six or seven years old she met on the streets of Calcutta. The little girl was literally living in a trash dump with her mother and siblings. Each day this little girl would crisscross the streets of the city looking for food. Mother Teresa decided to bring her to the

Missionaries of Charity children's home where she would receive shelter, food, and care.

The only problem was that the little girl would run away. The sisters would see her during the day and bring her back to the orphanage. But in the evening, without fail, the girl would find a way out and head back to the streets. Mother Teresa told the sisters to follow the girl to see where she was going. Mother Teresa remembered:

> The sister found the child sitting with her mother and sister under a tree. There was a little dish there and the mother was cooking food she had picked up from the streets. . . . And then we understood why the child ran away. The mother just loved the child. And the child loved the mother. They were so beautiful to each other. The child said *"bari jabo"*—it was her home. Her mother was her home.

Love is different from any other kind of relationship—even friendship—because a love relationship can be so devoted, even in the most trying situations or even if it is one-sided. You can love someone who may never return your love. Or a parent will always love a wayward child, no matter how selfish or uninterested or mean the child is. Parents continue to love them.

This was certainly the case in the relationship between St. Monica and her son, Augustine. Monica was a mother who witnessed Augustine turn his back on his Catholic faith. He lived an immoral life, fathering a son out of wedlock and living with a mistress. When Augustine came home from Rome to visit Monica in Carthage in North Africa, she refused to let him eat at her table or even sleep in her house. But she did not abandon him.

Monica had a vision in which she was standing on a wooden beam crying over her son's behavior. A ray of light came to her and asked why she was crying. In the vision she heard a voice say, "Your son is with you." When Monica told Augustine about the vision he said, "You see. I can come home." He said it would be easy to be reunited if she were to just give up her faith. Monica promptly answered, "The voice did not say that I was with you; it said that you were with me."

For years, Monica also sought out advice about her son. A bishop friend told her that it was better to talk to God about Augustine than to Augustine about God. He also said, "At present the heart of the young man is too stubborn, but God's time will come. It is not possible that the son of so many tears should perish."

When he was older, Augustine listened to the preaching of another bishop, St. Ambrose, and the light of the gospel finally reached his heart. He was baptized. Monica became sick shortly afterward. Before she died she told her son, "All I wished to live for was that I might see you a Catholic and a child of Heaven." You might also be interested to know that Augustine himself went on to be ordained, become a bishop, and is one of the greatest theologians the Church has ever known. And he is a saint himself! He and Monica share back-to-back feast days on August 27 and August 28!

That is the thing about love: it is boundless. When you commit to loving yourself, others, and God, all things are possible.

DIFFERENT WAYS TO LOVE

Making a commitment to love self, others, and God is the essential element of being a follower of Jesus Christ. As you think about the commitment to love, take some time to reacquaint yourself with the different ways to love.

I just mentioned one kind of love, filial love. This is the kind of love of a child for a parent, or vice versa. It is also the love you might have for a friend or someone you especially admire, like an older neighbor or a special teacher who has been important in your life. This kind of love is very loyal and can last throughout a lifetime. But it does not involve any romantic feelings.

There are love relationships connected with romantic feelings. But you have to be careful here, because romantic feelings are also commonly associated with infatuations. You probably have heard someone say, or said it yourself several times, "I love that guy" or "I love that girl" even though you may barely know him or her. You can be infatuated with people you don't even know and who don't even know you exist.

Infatuations are harmless as long as you don't make poor choices from them. On the other hand, you can be obsessed with someone you are infatuated with to the point that it pulls your entire life to a halt. You can't do your schoolwork. You don't talk with your parents. You ignore even your best friends. Even more risky, infatuations can cause people to make poor decisions and act out sexually in ways that are sinful.

You can tell the difference between a love relationship and an infatuation by looking at several qualities that will always be present in one but not necessarily the other.

Win it All

With true love, there is commitment. Love doesn't blow like the wind. It will survive tragedies, illness, and disagreements. There is also forgiveness in a love relationship. You can say to someone you love "I am sorry" and ask for his or her forgiveness. There is the opportunity for reconciliation. People who love each other also respect each other. They encourage each other to reach their true potential and to use their God-given gifts.

True love lasts. Don't forget some other elements of true love:

> Love is patient, love is kind.
> it is not jealous, [love] is not pompous, it
>   is not inflated,
> it is not rude,
> it does not seek its own interests,
> it is not quick-tempered,
> it does not brood over injury,
> it does not rejoice over wrongdoing but
>   rejoices with the truth.
> It bears all things, believes all things,
>   hopes all things, endures all things.
> Love never fails. (1 Cor 13:4–8b)

A phrase I use constantly is "Love is no matter what!" Jesus loves us no matter what, and he asks us to love no matter what the cost. This could mean separating yourself from people until they get their acts together. Even if you are apart from someone you love, you need to pray for and lead his or her by your own example.

YOUR COMMITMENT TO LOVE

Certainly any of the Christian vocations that you will commit your life to involve love. Think first of the vocation of marriage. In the sacrament of Matrimony, the couple is given the gift of unconditional love. The sacrament and marriage itself are indissoluble. The man and woman are given the grace to love each other in the same way that Christ loved the Church. They remain faithful to each other until death. They are blessed with a family and given the grace to raise their children. And they are also given the grace to remain faithful in their union until death.

At your age, whether you will be married or not, the model of married love is one you should practice and emulate in your own relationships. When I gave my life to Christ, one of the promises I made to myself was that if I were to get married in the future, I promised to behave honestly and honorably with *all women* until my wife came into my life. This practice also helped me to keep my life focused on Heaven. I did not want to act in any way that would be against the life I expected to live in eternity. There are several things you can do in this regard.

You can practice loyalty in your friendships. Do you have a long-time or family friend who isn't a part of your current friendship group? For whatever reason, you two have grown apart when it comes time to doing things together. Even if you don't hang out regularly, what's to keep you from scheduling some time together and going out for a meal or a movie with this person? This effort to maintain an old friendship will serve you well. It will help you to understand the meaning of loyalty and to appreciate relationships that stretch over time and weather changes in circumstances.

You can practice chastity. Chastity is the virtue in which you integrate your sexuality into your whole self, body, and spirit. Chastity helps you to control your sexual desires and use them appropriately according to your state in life. For you, this involves refraining from sex outside of marriage. This can be difficult given the culture that promotes random and impersonal sexual acts. But the rewards are great. You will be saving yourself for the benefits of true love and commitment of a holy marriage. When I was a junior in high school, Fr. Larry Richards challenged the boys to be the best examples of chastity. He would say, "Gentlemen, do not go below the neck until you are married." This blunt, simple advice was accurate and true. Any unchaste behavior you participate in before marriage will remain in your mind and in your psyche and damage your relationship with your future spouse. I soon realized that I should date only women I could envision myself marrying some day.

You can practice your faith. A married couple mirrors the love Christ had for his Church. Since you do not have a spouse now, you can mirror the love you may experience in reverse by developing a deep love for Jesus and the Church. Take a deep commitment and love for scripture, prayer, the sacraments, morality, and Church teaching with you into a relationship with a spouse. The more you each model the love of Christ for the Church, the deeper your own love will be for one another.

These elements of committed love also apply to the vocations of priesthood, consecrated life, and the committed single life. It's all about love that is committed, true, and rooted in the love God has for you. And it is love that stays with us and follows us into eternity!

UNENDING LOVE

Of all the things your mind has been created by God to understand, comprehending God's infinite and everlasting nature is among the most difficult. How can God have no beginning or end? What does it mean that God always was, always is, and always will be? How is this so?

This mystery cannot be fully revealed to our small and limited human minds. But you can begin to understand a little more of God's eternal nature by continuing to make the connection between God and love. "God is love, and whoever remains in love remains in God and God in him" (1 Jn 4:16). If it seems impossible to imagine how God has no beginning or no end, is it easier for you to understand when you substitute "love" for "God"? Love is eternal. Has there ever been a time in your own life when there has been an absence of love? Will there ever be?

God has revealed himself to you as a God of love, who himself is "an eternal exchange of love, Father, Son, and Holy Spirit" (*Catechism of the Catholic Church*, 221). You are destined to share in this love of God, in this life on earth and beyond.

God shared the revelation of his love gradually through history before fully revealing himself by sending his Son, Jesus Christ. In Jesus, God became flesh and walked among us. In the living gospel, Jesus showed by his words and actions how much love he has for you.

By committing to love of yourself and others, you are following through on Jesus' command to love God. But I want to conclude this step by mentioning another way to commit to love for the Lord: it is through your participation in the sacraments of the Church, especially the Eucharist. Jesus is truly present in the consecrated species of bread and wine that are his body and blood. When you celebrate Mass and receive holy communion, you are moving beyond the constraints of living in this world to anticipate your life of unending love in the next world.

I also want to point out one other phenomenon I have witnessed among many teens your age that is taking place more often today: Eucharistic adoration. For example, at a recent national youth ministry conference in Kansas City, Missouri, Mass was celebrated by more than 21,000 teenagers. But they didn't stop there! After Mass, they spent time in worship and adoration of the Lord in the Blessed Sacrament and then marched in a Eucharistic procession through the streets of Kansas City. It was powerful!

Similarly, the change of my life came on a particular Saturday night at a retreat called Teens Encounter Christ. There I sat in front of the Eucharist where Jesus was calling me to change. I heard him say to me, "If I commit to loving you by dying for you on a bloody cross, then why can't you give it all for me?" From that time on, any free time I have, I look for ways to be with Jesus in the Blessed Sacrament. When I was a teacher at Paramus Catholic High School, I would go to 6:30

a.m. Mass at Our Lady of Mount Carmel Church in Ridge-wood, New Jersey, and I would remain after to spend time in prayer. Soon I had many people coming with me. Some of the greatest conversions I have ever witnessed—including of my friend Paul who is now in the seminary—arose from those early morning times with the Lord.

My life is wonderful and a blessing, and it is because of the Lord. It is not because of money, cars, hobbies, partying with friends, or traveling the nation. My life is great because of the power of the Holy Eucharist. I like to say to people, "YOU ARE AMAZING!" I want them to know that they *are* amazing, but only because JESUS IS AMAZING! Jesus is the source of all blessings. When you come to realize this is so, your life will be such a gift. Loving Jesus with all your heart is the essence of winning it all.

My suggestion to you is this: reserve some time for personal prayer and adoration each week before the Blessed Sacrament. Look for a chapel or church with a tabernacle and sanctuary light (red candle) that is lit. This is your sign that Jesus is truly present there. Sit with him. Let him look at you and truly examine your heart and soul while you do the same self-reflection. Talk with him. And then, more importantly, listen to Jesus. St. Thérèse of Lisieux once said, "Do you realize that Jesus is there in the tabernacle expressly for you—for you alone? He burns with desire to come into your heart."

Seek the Lord where he can be found in the Blessed Sacrament. Love him. Let him show his love for you!

Most importantly, "LOVE 'EM ALWAYS" just as Jesus did!

Questions to Help You Win It All

1. How can you love yourself without being self-centered?

2. What is unconditional love?

3. How do you understand the difference between unconditional love and infatuation?

4. What are other ways you can model the virtue of love?

5. How do you understand the infinite nature of God's love?

STEPS TO COMMIT TO LOVING

- Reserve time to participate in a weekday Mass. Allow for some extra time to remain in church for quiet prayer and reflection before the Blessed Sacrament.

- Spend at least five minutes in silence every day listening to God. Let his love fill you up!

- Pray for the persons who have hurt you the most. Pray for them in love. God never said for you to make your enemies your friends. He only asked you to love them.

Seven⁷

Never Give Up

REAL INSPIRATION

When I went on ABC's *Nightline* a few years ago, John Donvan, the interviewer, asked me, "Why do you sound like Rocky Balboa? Are you from Philadelphia or something?" I answered "No!"

"Then why *do* you sound like Rocky?" I had to laugh to myself when I thought of the reason. I said, "Well, John, I am from Erie, Pennsylvania, a town about five hundred miles from Philadelphia. The reason I sound like Rocky is because every time at a young age when I felt like giving up, I would draw strength from him."

Really, that is exactly what I would do. I even remember my brother saying to me when I was about fifteen, "You do know that Rocky is not real. Right?"

Nevertheless, I would come home from school, maybe after getting a detention or failing a test, and put on one of the Rocky movies—from the original all the way to *Rocky IV.* (*Rocky V* is weak!) Whatever it was about them, the Rocky story taught me to never give up. I took to heart that I, too, could accomplish some great things in life as long as I have hope like my man Rocky.

As I grew up, I realized that there was someone else in my life who was a true and real model of perseverance, courage, and strength. This person, my Lord and God, Jesus Christ, never gave up his mission to save the world from sin. And he never gives up on me, despite my own sinfulness.

I love Jesus! I hope you love him, too!

JESUS' COMMITMENT TO YOU

In fact, I soon learned, the most extreme and ultimate example of someone "never giving up" comes from the Lord himself.

Jesus was commissioned by God the Father for a one-of-a-kind mission: the redemption of the world. Through the life he shared with Mary and Joseph in Nazareth, through his relationship with his disciples and his ministry to the poor and lowly, Jesus had a clear sense of what he was called to do.

And he did not give up until he had reached his goal. He could have said, "This is too hard" or "Even if I do this, people won't change their lives." Instead, he said, "Yes! You are worth it. You are on my mind when I go through this pain. I will never give up on you!"

The last hours of his life offer some key lessons for you as you work to develop a deep sense of commitment to being a disciple of Christ.

In the garden of Gethsemane, Jesus could have easily given up. What despair he must have felt knowing what was ahead. He said, "My soul is sorrowful even to death" (Mk 14:34). Jesus even prayed to his Father that the pain he knew he must endure could be removed. Yet he roused himself and his friends to get up and go to the place where he knew he would be betrayed and arrested.

A first lesson for you to remain persistent in your life's calling is to **pray always.** Before he was crucified, Jesus called to his Father again in prayer. His words were not self-serving. They were not a call for rescue. Rather, Jesus said, "Father, forgive them, they know not what they do" (Lk 23:24). Jesus was praying for his enemies, the ones who nailed him to the cross. He was hung between two common criminals. He prayed for them, too, telling one of them "Amen, I say to you, today you will be with me in Paradise" (Lk 23:43).

And then, just before he died, Jesus looked down from the cross and saw his beloved friend, John, and his mother, Mary. He addressed them and reminded them to care for each other: "Woman, behold your son," he said to Mary. To John he said, "Behold, your mother" (Jn 19:26–27).

A second lesson to help you to never give up in pursuing your goals and mission for life is to **accept help from others.** The pain that Jesus dealt with in being scourged, crowned with thorns, and forced to carry a cross through the narrow streets of Jerusalem to the hill of Golgotha outside of the city was infinitely more of a physical challenge than any faced by any pro athlete or any extreme sport reality show star today. Though a person condemned by a Roman court was expected to bear his own instrument of torture, the soldiers "pressed into service a passer-by, Simon, a Cyrenian . . . to carry his cross" (Mk 15:21). There is nothing in the Gospels about how Jesus resisted Simon's help, about how he had to "go it alone," or about how his pride in accomplishing his goal "on his own" got in the way of accepting help from a passer-by.

A third lesson about the importance of never giving up involves your motivation. Stay committed and continue to push yourself to reach your goals **because your family, friends, and even your enemies need you to do so.** Let's take some time to look at these three lessons in a little more detail.

PRAY ALWAYS

Prayer is a long conversation with God! Many people think prayer is only a time to recite a bunch of words and to address a set of needs to God. It is much more than that. To be a committed pray-er, you first have to realize that prayer really involves much more *listening* than *talking.*

In the listening part, you allow God to speak to you through your intellect, feelings, imagination, will, and memories. In order to be able to hear God speak to you in these ways, you have to be able to quiet yourself enough to be able to hear him.

I've been on a silent retreat before. Do you know what that is? I went to a monastery and spent some time with the monks. I was prohibited from speaking out loud for thirty hours. Even if you barely know me, you would know how difficult that was for me! But it was also very freeing. I learned so much from the experience. I was able to hear God inspiring me to new things, helping to recognize what is important in my life, and healing some bad memories that had been bothering me.

To pray well, you have to find some time to calm yourself and to relax. It doesn't have to happen at a monastery or only on special occasions. Make a commitment to reserve part of each day to sit still, relax, free your mind of all unnecessary thoughts, and to ready yourself for a deeper connection with the Lord.

I have another suggestion for your prayer time. Look for variation! You don't always have to pray in the same ways. Maybe your family has the practice of reciting a decade or more of the rosary each night. This is great! But did you ever think of other ways you can pray the rosary? How about a "rosary run" where you begin your meditation on part of one mystery—say, the first sorrowful mystery, Jesus in the Garden —and then run one lap around a quarter-mile track as you say ten Hail Marys to yourself? After a lap, pause, reflect, and repeat the process with another of the mysteries.

There are other bold and new ways to pray. Have you ever prayed out loud in public? In working with teenagers and their youth groups over the years, I have been with them in restaurants when we will also say in one loud, united voice a prayer before eating. You should see the stares we get from other people in the restaurant. It even feels like some of the people are mad at us for praying! I always point out to the teens that no one thinks its weird when football players come out of the tunnel before games making all kinds of grunting, hissing noises to get themselves ready for the action because that is what football players do. No one should think it strange to hear Christians praying in public, especially asking for a blessing on the meal. Praying is what Christians do!

You probably already know a lot about praying. You probably have memorized many different prayers. In whatever way you choose to pray, you must be open to God's presence. Approach him with humility. Believe that he will be with you during your time in prayer.

Don't ever give up your commitment to pray, even when it gets difficult. Distractions are bound to occur, and your commitment may be less strong. You may be lazy or tired. Also, Satan will tempt you in many ways to get you to ignore your time for prayer. Even if you do reserve time to pray, you may think that God is not listening to you and that your prayers are not answered. The Lord answers all of your prayers in his own time and way. In order to never give up your prayer life, you must keep the faith that God always hears you, even if you do not "feel" anything. When things seem to be going poorly, pray to the Holy Spirit to come to you. Fight through and continue to make time for prayer.

Jesus does not want you to give up in your prayer life! He wants you to model your prayer life on the parable of the persistent widow (see Luke 18:1–8). Do you remember how the parable goes? A widow in town approached a dishonest judge over and over for him to render a just decision in a legal case. Only because the widow kept bothering him did the judge deliver a just decision for her. Jesus concluded the parable with this teaching:

> Pay attention to what the dishonest judge says. Will not God then secure the rights of his chosen ones who call out to him day and night? Will he be slow to answer them? I tell you, he will see to it that justice is done for them speedily.

Jesus then adds, "But when the Son of Man comes, will he find any faith on earth?" Make sure that if Jesus returns to earth today, he finds you at prayer and faith-filled!

ACCEPT HELP FROM OTHERS

A version of an old but meaningful story was told around the time of the tragic Hurricane Katrina that struck the area around New Orleans in 2004.

The way the story goes, a man got word of the impending hurricane and began to pray to God to save him from disaster.

Soon afterward, the first rescuers arrived in a large van, knocked on the man's door, and told him to get in the van. The neighborhood was being evacuated. "Oh, no," the man said, "I will stay right here. God will save me."

The rains and wind soon became a flood as the levies broke and water poured into the city. The man continued to pray. His street was like a river and water gushed into his home, causing him to retreat to the upper floor. The next rescuer arrived in a large rubber boat with a separate seat in the back to take the man to safety. "Here, get in the boat," the rescuer said, "the waters are rising. This may be your last chance to escape." The man turned his back and climbed the last of the dry stairs heading up to the attic. He said again, "I don't need your help. I will stay right here. God will save me."

The man's prayers increased as the water filled his house. He escaped to the roof and could literally feel the foundation of the house swaying under the strong current of water below. It wasn't too long after that a police helicopter hovered above him. A basket and a harness were dropped from above with a trained officer to help the man get in it and fasten up. When the officer got low enough to shout instructions, the man shouted back in an even louder voice, "Go away! I told them already, I don't need any of your help. God will save me!"

Of course, in the story's last scene the man comes face to face with God and asks him, "How could you have let me die? I prayed constantly for my rescue. Why didn't you answer me?"

And God says, "I did answer you. I sent you a large van, a rubber boat, and a helicopter with a harness and a rescue basket. You weren't paying attention."

The message of the story is probably easy for you to see: God uses the people in our lives to answer our prayers and fulfill our needs. Be ready to accept help from others in your own life!

Think about people who have influenced your own faith life. Certainly, your parents have had an effect in several different ways, both concrete and implied. Have your parents practiced their religion? Have they made it a family habit of praying together? Have they shared lessons about Christ, the gospel, and the Church with you? Whether you answered yes or no to those questions, your parents have influenced your understanding of God and your practice of religion right now. If you have come from a family where religion is central, you may now be looking for new ways to make your faith your own as you grow into adulthood. If you answered "no" to the questions above, the lack of formal religious experience may be moving you to learn more about God and to cultivate a deeper relationship with him.

Look also to people in your life right now for encouragement to keep the commitment to a growing faith. How have Catholic friends inspired you? Who are teachers who have awakened a desire to take on the Gospel? How has the holy example of a priest, sister, or brother been a model for you?

Continue to draw on these mentors to support you in your pursuit of a life of committed Christian discipleship. Remember, we are one body in Christ. Accept the help of others with the same enthusiasm that you share your own gifts with everyone you meet!

OTHER PEOPLE NEED YOU—EVEN YOUR ENEMIES!

You've likely seen the movie *It's A Wonderful Life* every year at Christmas. It packs a clear message: everyone's life has meaning. In the story, George Bailey's guardian angel, Clarence, painstakingly points out to George how the lives of his family, neighbors, and even enemies would have been different (worse) if he had never been born. Probably one of the reasons this movie is a classic and plays every year on network television is that this strong and positive message is something everyone feels good about hearing.

Your life, too, is of top-shelf importance. You can have a positive and necessary influence on many people. Your commitment to follow Jesus Christ and to practice your Catholic faith is an inspiration to all, especially many of your peers, who may be distant from God and religion. That is why it is so important that you never give up in your quest to win it all and gain Heaven. This is a goal that not only benefits you, it is one that could have vital importance to the other people around you. Wouldn't be great to know that you helped others gain the joys of Heaven?

In addition to inspiring others by your Christian life, your very efforts can affect the chances that family, friends, and enemies will have to know and love Jesus and live with him in eternity.

Recall again the ancient practice in the Church known as "offering it up." What this means is that you can give to the Lord your efforts, works, joys, and sufferings for the benefit of another. You can do this informally by saying to yourself something like, "Jesus, use this pain I am experiencing for the salvation of my friend (or brother, parent, enemy, etc.)." This practice of offering up our works and challenges also benefits the souls of purgatory so that they may someday even sooner be united with God in the fullness of Heaven.

Please don't forget that your enemies need you, too. If someone tells me he or she can't stand me, I only want to love him or her even more.

At the beginning of the discussion of this step, I mentioned a fictional hero of mine, Rocky Balboa. Now I want to share with you the story of two real-life baseball players who bring inspiration. These two men were once enemies but in the end needed each other.

Juan Marichal was a pitcher for the San Francisco Giants. John Roseboro was a catcher for the hated rival Los Angeles Dodgers. When the teams met in a late summer game in San Francisco nearly fifty years ago, both teams were battling for first place.

Marichal was accused in the game of intentionally trying to hit some of the Dodgers with his pitches. The Dodgers were upset, and Roseboro decided to take the matter into his own hands. When Marichal was up to bat, Roseboro tried to hit him with the ball as he threw it back to the pitcher.

What happened next was one of the ugliest incidents to ever take place in a major league baseball game. Marichal spun around and began to attack Roseboro using his bat as a weapon. The catcher was struck in the head, opening up a large gash. A fourteen-minute fight between the teams followed. In the aftermath, Juan Marichal received a suspension and a large fine.

Now skip ahead to a time when both players had retired from playing. Juan Marichal had a record as one of the best pitchers to have ever played baseball. He deserved to be in the Baseball Hall of Fame. But because of the incident with John Roseboro, he was passed over in the voting the first four years he was on the ballot.

Win it All

In his fifth year of eligibility and seventeen years after he struck John Roseboro with a bat, Juan Marichal received some help from an unlikely source. John Roseboro himself wrote a public letter in support of Marichal's election into the Hall of Fame. "There were not hard feelings on my part, "said Roseboro. "Over the years, you learn to forget things."

After Roseboro's public support, Juan Marichal was elected into the Baseball Hall of Fame the following year.

In his Letter to the Romans, St. Paul wrote, "We, though many, are one body in Christ and individually parts of one another" (Rom 12:5).

You are needed by family, friends, and even your enemies. Without his "enemy," Juan Marichal might not have reached the Hall of Fame. Never give up on drawing yourself into a deeper relationship with Christ and the Church. It is essential. You are needed.

Questions to Help You Win It All

1. How does Christ himself inspire you to "never give up"?

2. What are some creative ways that you have prayed?

3. Who are people God has sent to you to influence your faith life?

4. What new motivation do you have to never give up the quest to be a better disciple of Christ?

5. How have you inspired another with your faith in Christ?

STEPS TO REMEMBER TO NEVER GIVE UP

- Anytime you feel like giving up, watch a movie that will inspire you. Some of my favorites beyond the *Rocky* series: *Rudy*, *Hoosiers*, *Remember the Titans*, and *The Blind Side*.

- Call a person this week and express your gratitude to him or her for being an encouragement to you.

- Offer each day to Christ. Begin by praying the Morning Offering (see page 138).

Eight

Live Every Day as If It Were Your Last

HERE TODAY

The April 15, 2009, edition of the Virginia Tech student newspaper, the *Collegiate Times*, remembered the horrific shootings that had taken place on the campus one year before. One article wondered what the life of one of the victims, Matthew La Porte, would have been like had he not been killed:

> Cadet Matthew La Porte would have woken up this morning with only a month to go until his graduation from the Virginia Tech Corps of Cadets.
>
> He'd also be one day closer to starting the dream career he'd diligently pursued in the Air Force ROTC program, serving his country as a second lieutenant intelligence officer.
>
> La Porte would have been up before the sun rose today, preparing his uniform, gray slacks with a white short-sleeved button-up shirt, in order to be ready for morning formation at 7:20 a.m. After, he'd grab a bit of breakfast . . . then a quick nap . . . before heading toward the Military Building.

Matthew had a reputation among his fellow cadets for liking to sleep and for being tardy to several commitments. "He was not a sterling cadet at everything," said one of his freshman and sophomore hallmates, "but the few things that he did, he did them real well."

Ultimately, Matthew La Porte was ready for his last day on earth. The reports from witnesses at the time of the tragic shooting said that Matthew was killed while trying to help get other people away from the shooter. Another of his friends said, "What some people call instinct, Matt simply acted on what he knew to be right."

Though never in a million years would Matt and the others shot and killed at Virginia Tech have imagined that a day that began with the routine of any other would have ended in their deaths, Matt certainly had lived a life that had prepared him for what happened. He truly modeled the goal of this eighth and final step: to "live every day as if it were your last."

I know for a fact that Matt was prepared for the incident that took his life because I was acquainted with him and his family personally through his younger sister, Priscilla, a four-year member of a youth group I ministered to in New Jersey.

He was a great kid. When he was in sixth grade, he told his parents he wanted to attend Carson Long Military Institute in Pennsylvania to help him boost his discipline and grades so that he could get into a good college. He had goals for his life that he remained committed to until his very last day.

When Matt died, I was living in Syracuse. His sister Priscilla called me on the phone in hysterics: "Fatica, you have to pray for me. My brother was one of the kids on the news who was shot. He is dead."

I hopped on a plane immediately and headed to Virginia Tech to pray with Priscilla and her family. This was something I had to do in order to be ready to live *my* vocation. It is what Priscilla needed and what was right. The story of Matthew La Porte certainly reminds us of the very real risks we face each day that we walk out into the world.

Not only do you need to be aware that each day could possibly be your last, but you have to think the same for those around you and treat them accordingly. You probably know of several people who have unexpectedly lost a parent or other relative due to something sudden like a heart attack or a car accident. How differently would you treat the people you are close to if you knew for a fact that they wouldn't be with you tomorrow?

Something like this happened to me recently. I ran into one of the teens I knew from a local high school in Syracuse one day at a Ruby Tuesday's restaurant. Her name was Corey, and she wanted me to share the table with her and her friends.

I told her I was there to have lunch with some other people and I couldn't sit with her. Instead, I wanted her to do me a favor. Would she join with some other teens from our youth group and go to a youth rally in Connecticut? She told me she would think about going along.

A few days later I was at Corey's high school to begin planning for a retreat. I saw Corey and gave her a permission slip for the trip. She looked at her friends and said, "Sorry, Justin. Maybe next time."

When I returned from the rally in Connecticut, I had a phone message to call the principal at Corey's school. It was urgent. I thought he was calling only about the retreat, which would begin in a couple of days. So thinking nothing more of it, I went to the principal's office. Even when I saw the principal and vice principal waiting for me with tears in their eyes, I couldn't have imagined the shocking news to come. "Justin," the principal began, "Corey Craig committed suicide last night."

The news was devastating. I thought of Corey and how I would never see her again. I beat myself up and thought if only Corey had been at the youth rally with us. What could I have done differently to help her? I thought of how she was counting on me. "My God, " I prayed, "this mission to follow You, Lord, is no joke."

I soon realized that there was another person who felt worse than me. His name was Alex. He told me that he broke Corey's heart eight months before. He said it was his fault that Corey was dead. I consoled him by saying that Corey made a very wrong decision that was hers alone. But Alex was still hurting badly. I told him to meet me at Mass the next morning and to bring a friend because we would be taking a ride after Mass.

We started driving, and Alex wondered where we were going. I told him we were going to see Corey's parents and that he was going to tell them he was sorry for their loss and also sorry that he had hurt Corey.

Alex was so fearful that Corey's parents would hate him and blame him. He knew that others were blaming him. When Corey's mom saw Alex sitting in the car she came running from the front porch to give him a hug. She told him that she could *never* hate him. He had made Corey happier than anything on earth. She told him that it wasn't his fault.

Corey's father was admittedly angry that morning. His beautiful daughter and only child had ended her life. It was true: Alex had broken her heart. He went back inside the house to collect his thoughts and decided how he would handle this first meeting with Alex since Corey's death.

This man did something I will never forget. Corey's dad came outside, approached Alex, and embraced him. He asked Alex to promise to make something of his life. He told Alex,

"My daughter didn't die for no reason. Alex, do good things with your life."

Corey's death was tragic. She made an awful choice that hurt so many people who loved her. But her father's words are correct: she did not die for no reason. Alex and I (and hopefully you, too) are reminded to be more aware of the people who are near to us and the hurt they are experiencing. You need to keep in mind the fragility of life. Either you or those close to you could be gone tomorrow.

WHAT HAPPENS AFTER YOU DIE?

Do you know what the Catholic Church teaches about suicide? The taking of one's own life is a serious evil that shows a total lack of self-love and a rejection of the God of life. Suicide also displays a serious lack of love of others. When suicide is intended to give a bad example, especially to other young people, it is an example of the worst kind of scandal.

However, many people who commit suicide are suffering from serious psychological problems. This may lessen the person's guilt before God for an action that is always objectively and gravely wrong. You don't have to judge the state of the person's soul before God. You should just pray for people who do this and ask God to have mercy on them.

The deaths of Matt and Corey and many other unexpected deaths of people who are close to you bring up the question "What happens to us after we die?"

One of the reasons you should live every day as if it were your last is so you can always be prepared to die a good death. Blessed Junípero Serra put it this way:

> A happy death of all the things of life is our
> principal concern. For if we attain that, it matters
> little if we lose all the rest. But if we do not attain
> that, nothing else will be of any value.

If sin had not entered the world, there would be no need to worry about death. We would have been freed from bodily death. With the entrance of sin into the world, this gift was taken away. Death became a natural part of human existence. As the Book of Ecclesiastes puts it:

> There is an appointed time for everything, and a
> time for every affair under the heavens. A time to be
> born, and a time to die. (Eccl 3:1–2)

It is natural to die, though death is a great mystery. We do know that Jesus has obliterated the power of death to be the end of life. Through the Son of God's own acceptance of death and his resurrection from the dead, we have hope that death is but an entrance into eternal life with the Father, Son, and Holy Spirit.

Have you heard my message about what it means to win it all? First, let me repeat what "winning it all" is *not* all about:

- collecting the most possessions
- having the most power
- hanging with only popular and cool people
- letting society define your success

What "winning it all" is all about is praying deeply to God to have mercy on you so that you can get to Heaven. But it is even more than that. We want our family and friends and enemies, too, to be with us in Heaven. Wouldn't that make Heaven even greater? So we need to win it all RIGHT NOW! Bow your head RIGHT NOW! Stop what you are doing and before you finish this book, pray for Heaven. Pray RIGHT NOW that your priorities are transformed. Pray for Heaven for yourself and those around you. This is what it means to win it all!

Yes, winning it all is about rising on the last day with Christ in his glory. But this can happen only if you die in union with him with no sin on your heart. You have one life to live and one death to experience; there is no reincarnation. Think about Jesus' words in the parable of the rich fool:

> There was a rich man whose land produced a bountiful harvest. He asked himself, "What shall I do, for I do not have space to store my harvest?" And he said, "This is what I shall do: I shall tear down my barns and build large ones. There I shall store all my grain and other goods and I shall say to myself, 'Now as for you, you have so many good things stored up for many years, rest, eat, drink be merry!'" But God said to him, "You fool, this night your life will be demanded of you; and the things you have prepared, to whom will they belong?" Thus will it be for the one who stores up treasure for himself but is not rich in what matters to God. (Lk 12:16–21)

The truth of living each day as your last is a powerful motivator to help you live a life of love and a life of purpose. St. John Vianney said, "Life is given to us that we may learn to die well, and we never think of it. To die well we must live well."

Keeping your own death in mind is a way to help you to a better life in the present. Have you ever thought about what you would do and what you would say if you believed that Christ would judge you in the next few hours? If you lived with this attitude, how well do you think you would do in attracting the people around you—friends and enemies alike—to the Lord Jesus and the good news of salvation?

YOUR PLAN FOR YOUR LAST DAY

The Sea of Galilee is really more of a large lake that was right in the middle of the place where Jesus lived and preached. Many times, Jesus set off by boat—likely a very primitive boat compared to those of today—to get from one side of the lake to the other. And he often asked his followers to get in the boat with him.

The water had to have been intimidating. Storms, waves, wind. It's doubtful that there were any life jackets on board. This wasn't an era where moms and dads took their kids down to the local pool for swimming lessons. There probably weren't too many on board with Jesus who could swim a lap across an Olympic-sized pool or even survive if they fell in the water.

And yet every day, many people did get on the boat with Jesus. They did head off to a place on the other side of the lake that was uncharted and strange to them, truly out of their comfort zone. Why? Because they believed in Jesus and his promise for new and eternal life. It was worth it to them to risk their lives in the present for a boundless life of happiness and joy in the future.

What does this mean for you right now? "Getting on the boat" with Jesus today means a daily commitment to following the Lord. Can you make a commitment to the following?

- I am willing to talk about my faith with my peers.
- I am willing to pray in public.
- I am willing to pray before every meal.
- I am willing to pray for my enemies and show them compassion and forgiveness.
- I am willing to read the Bible daily.
- I am willing to avoid destructive behaviors like drinking alcohol, using drugs, and having sex outside of marriage.
- I am willing to get away from people who gossip.
- I am willing to tell people who use God's name in vain to stop.
- I am willing to stop swearing.
- I am willing to live honestly, including never cheating on schoolwork.
- I am willing to commit to going to Mass each Sunday and holy day, no matter if someone tells me to or not.

Sure, there are many obstacles to getting on the boat with Jesus and living each day as if it were your last. But don't forget, you do not have to go it alone. Jesus is with you. I mean he is *really* with you. That brings up the way I would like to live the day if I knew it were my last. It is the way I would like to live every day. I try to live one day at a time so that I don't get ahead of myself. Go ahead, put one foot in front of the other, and give it all you've got each day!

JESUS' PRESENCE IN THE EUCHARIST

I love watching football. It has truly become America's game. One of the things that is different about modern football than in years past is the innovations that take place on offense. I can barely keep up with all of the terminology, from trips and wildcat formations to spread offenses.

Back when Vince Lombardi coached the Green Bay Packers to five NFL championships and wins in the first two Super Bowls, his offense was much simpler. In fact, it was said that Coach Lombardi's teams ran two basic plays—sweep left and sweep right—with only small variations. In order to make these plays work, the coach had his team practice them over and over so that every player did his job just right and so the play would come off to near perfection. Even then, Coach Lombardi's players said that his practices were never dull. He had a way of making the most mundane chores seem fresh and new.

Vince Lombardi was a lifelong Catholic. He played football for and graduated from Fordham University. When he was a little boy, he wanted to be a priest. Throughout his life, no matter how busy he was, he reserved part of his day for daily Mass. As in football practice, Coach Lombardi believed that success in faith came with daily practice. He chose this occasion to be with Jesus in the Eucharist.

I agree wholeheartedly with this great coach. There is no better way to spend any day—and especially a day you are living as if it were your last—with Jesus in the sacrament of the Holy Eucharist. Make it a plan to go to Mass as much as possible.

When the Catholic bishops met in Rome at the Second Vatican Council in the 1960s, a good deal of their time and energy was spent in praying over and discussing the Eucharist. They agreed that the Eucharist is the "source and summit of Christian life." This means that our lives have their origin in Jesus, who is truly present in the consecrated bread and wine, and that there is nothing we can do bigger or better than to share in his presence at Mass.

If I had one day to live, there is no doubt that I would spend that day with Jesus in the celebration of the holy Mass. The saints agree with me! For example:

> If you ate only one meal a week, would you survive? It is the same for your soul. Nourish it with the Blessed Sacrament.
>
> —Bl. Brother André Bessette

> I can no longer live without Jesus. How soon shall I receive him again?
>
> —St. Maria Goretti

> Our Lord does not come down from Heaven every day to lie in a golden ciborium. He comes to find another Heaven which is infinitely dearer to him— the Heaven of our souls.
>
> —St. Thérèse of Lisieux

> Holy Communion is the shortest and safest way to Heaven. There are others: innocence, but that is for little children; penance, but we are afraid of it;

generous endurance of trials of life, but when they come we weep and ask to be spared. The surest, easiest, shortest way is the Eucharist.

—St. Pius X

These words of the saints remind us that our home is in Heaven. Our time on earth is temporary and fleeting. Just imagine how your life on earth will be measured in proportion to life in eternity—truly a drop in the bucket in comparison! Your goal is Heaven. Don't ever forget it. Live every day keeping that goal in mind.

Never forget that today could be your last.

Never forget why you are on earth.

Never forget your purpose in life.

Never forget that you are only here to WIN IT ALL!

Questions to Help You Win It All

1. How would you treat people differently if you knew that they would die tomorrow?

2. What would you consider to be a "happy death"?

3. How would you spend your last day on earth if you knew that you were about to die?

4. What is the greatest obstacle to you "getting in the boat" with Jesus?

STEPS TO LIVE EVERY DAY AS IF IT WERE YOUR LAST

- Give your life to Christ. Say the Mary the Mother of God Surrender Prayer (see page 140).

- Hang a crucifix in your room at home. When you look at Jesus on the cross, surrender all your fears and worries to him.

- Like Vince Lombardi, commit to going to daily Mass as often as possible. Set a regular day each week to attend a weekday Mass at a nearby Catholic church.

Afterword

I t was Fr. Jonathan Kalisch, O.P., who told me I had to watch an amazing HBO documentary about Justin Fatica—a guy who ministered to young people in an apostolate called Hard as Nails. We sat down and watched it together, and I was mesmerized by this young man who exuded such an overwhelming conviction about Jesus Christ and the realness of his mercy. And I remember wishing that I could be more like that myself.

It wasn't long after that Fr. Jonathan invited Justin to give a Hard as Nails mission at Quinnipiac University, where Fr. Jonathan was the chaplain. During that time, Justin stayed with us at Saint Mary's Priory in New Haven, Connecticut. When I met him in person, that same conviction for the Gospel came through, along with a powerful humility, passion, simplicity, and Justin's trademark intensity. When you are in Justin's presence, you feel the closeness of Christ.

Justin and Fr. Jonathan went off to begin the mission on the Quinnipiac campus. For the most part, the students had never heard of Justin Fatica. But word got around about what was happening through this extraordinary man who was there proclaiming Jesus Christ. And at one of the mission events more than four hundred students showed up needing to be part of what was going on. When I heard that, I was awestruck. In my experience, getting young people excited about religion is one of the most difficult tasks on earth. But here it was taking place in a practically miraculous way. Why? I believe it is because of the unique humanity of Justin Fatica. The young people who heard Justin speak found in him Jesus Christ, the One they had always been waiting for.

Justin is a man who is totally given over to Jesus Christ. And not just to Christ's *message*; he is given over to the Person of Christ. He knows Jesus as a flesh-and-blood friend. When he speaks about Jesus Christ, he speaks about someone with a voice and with a face—someone you can meet and who wants to meet you. It's clear to me that Christ has called Justin to be a unique witness to the world in order to share that Jesus Christ is real, he is alive, he wants to be known, and he wants to be involved in our lives—especially in the places where our lives are most falling apart. Jesus wants to come close to us through the pain we experience. He wants to heal us through his wounds.

Personally, I would never ever believe that such a thing were possible or imaginable if I didn't actually experience it through the witness of someone who was so different, and so attractive, and so utterly committed that I couldn't deny it. That's what happens when you meet Justin Fatica. He lives to save souls. He calls you out of hiding. He helps you to face the things in your life that most terrorize you, that hold you hostage, that fill you with fear, shame, sorrow, or hopelessness. And then he shows you that there is Someone greater than the sum total of those things, Someone who understands you completely and who desires to come close to you as your Savior and your Friend. Nothing—no evil on earth, no pain, no problem, no hurt, or suffering—is greater than the healing and the forgiveness and the tenderness of Jesus Christ.

How many young people has Justin helped to release from the bondage of their own despair? Justin tells the story of a boy who, in a rage, held a knifepoint murderously against Justin's neck. Justin's response was, "Kill me right now. But even if you do, I will still love you." Really? There is actually someone in the world who responds to hatred and violence with love? That's someone I have to get know, because I need to become like him. Whatever makes him that way has to take over my life as well. I want to live that different humanity. That's what knowing Justin makes you pray. I'm very grateful to God to know Justin Fatica.

Fr. Peter John Cameron, O.P.

More
Helps to
Win It All

CREEDS
Apostles' Creed

I believe in God,
    the Father almighty,
    creator of heaven and earth.

I believe in Jesus Christ
    his only Son, Our Lord.

He was conceived by the
    power of the Holy Spirit
    and born of the Virgin Mary.

He suffered under Pontius Pilate,
    was crucified, died, and was buried.
    He descended into hell.

On the third day he rose again.

He ascended into heaven
    and is seated at the right
    hand of the Father.
    He will come again to judge
    the living and the dead.

I believe in the Holy Spirit,
    the holy catholic Church,
    the communion of saints,
    the forgiveness of sins,
    the resurrection of the body,
    and the life everlasting.
    Amen.

Nicene Creed

We believe in one God,
the Father, the Almighty,
maker of heaven and earth,
of all that is seen and unseen.
We believe in one Lord, Jesus Christ,
the only Son of God,
eternally begotten of the Father,
God from God, Light from Light,
true God from true God,
begotten, not made, one in Being with the Father.
Through him all things were made.
For us men and for our salvation
he came down from heaven:
by the power of the Holy Spirit
he was born of the Virgin Mary, and became man.
For our sake he was crucified under Pontius Pilate;
he suffered, died, and was buried.
On the third day he rose again in fulfillment of the
Scriptures;
he ascended into heaven and is seated at the right
hand of the Father.
He will come again in glory to judge the living and
the dead,
and his kingdom will have no end.
We believe in the Holy Spirit, the Lord, the giver of life,
who proceeds from the Father and the Son.
With the Father and the Son he is worshiped and
glorified.
He has spoken through the Prophets.

We believe in one holy catholic and apostolic Church.
We acknowledge one baptism for the forgiveness of sins.
We look for the resurrection of the dead,
and the life of the world to come. Amen.

HOW TO GO TO CONFESSION

1. Spend some time examining your conscience (see list of sins on pages 123–125). Consider your actions and attitudes in each area of your life (e.g., faith, family, school/work, social life, relationships). Ask yourself, "Is this area of my life pleasing to God? What needs to be reconciled with God? With others? With myself?"

2. Sincerely tell God that you are sorry for your sins. Ask God for forgiveness and for the grace you will need to change what needs changing in your life. Promise God that you will try to live according to his will for you.

3. Approach the area for confession. Wait an appropriate distance until it is your turn.

4. Make the Sign of the Cross with the priest. He may say, "May God, who has enlightened every heart, help you to know your sins and trust his mercy." You reply, "Amen."

5. Confess your sins to the priest. Simply and directly talk to him about the areas of sinfulness in your life that need God's healing touch.

6. The priest will ask you to pray an Act of Contrition. Pray an Act of Contrition you have committed to memory (see page 139). Or say something in your own words, like "Dear God, I am sorry for my sins. I ask for your forgiveness, and I promise to do better in the future."

7. The priest will talk to you about your life, encourage you to be more faithful to God in the future, and help you decide what to do to make up for your sins—your penance.

8. The priest will then extend his hands over your head and pray the Church's official prayer of absolution:

> God, the Father of mercies, through the Death and Resurrection of his Son, has reconciled the world to himself and sent the Holy Spirit among us for the forgiveness of sins; through the ministry of the Church may God give you pardon and peace, and I absolve you from your sins in the name of the Father, and of the Son, and of the Holy Spirit.

You respond, "Amen."

9. The priest will wish you peace. Thank him and leave.

10. Go to a quiet place in church and pray your prayer of penance. Then spend some time quietly thanking God for the gift of forgiveness.

Examination of Conscience

You may wish to put a check by those sins you should confess. This list is provided at the courtesy of Fr. Larry Richards (see: www.thereasonforourhope.org/pdfs/14.pdf).

❑ abortion

❑ adultery

❑ all use of illegal drugs

❑ any dealing with the occult (ouija boards, etc.)

❑ artificial birth control

Win it All

- ❏ blasphemy (disrespect toward God's holy name)
- ❏ breaking promises deliberately
- ❏ bringing dishonor to school, family, or church
- ❏ calumny (telling lies about another)
- ❏ despair (to refuse God's offer of forgiveness or help)
- ❏ destruction of other people's property
- ❏ detraction (telling an unkind truth about another)
- ❏ disobedience toward parents and teachers
- ❏ drunkenness at any time in life, including any underage drinking
- ❏ excessive materialism
- ❏ gluttony (eating or drinking in excess)
- ❏ gossip (talking about others)
- ❏ hatred
- ❏ homosexual actions
- ❏ impure thoughts
- ❏ indifference between good or evil
- ❏ ingratitude
- ❏ intentional violation of the rules (school or law)
- ❏ jealousy
- ❏ laziness

❑ lying

❑ malice (the deliberate choice of evil)

❑ masturbation (impure actions with yourself)

❑ missing Mass on Sunday or any of the holy days

❑ murder

❑ not praying every day

❑ not giving to the poor and the church

❑ premarital sex (including intercourse, oral sex, and impure touching of another)

❑ presumption (sinning and saying God must forgive you)

❑ pride

❑ prostitution

❑ reckless driving that endangers yourself or others

❑ rudeness

❑ selfishness

❑ stealing

❑ superstition

❑ unjustified anger

❑ using others for your own personal gain

❑ watching or looking at pornographic material

Win ^{it} All

DEVOTIONS
The Rosary

Joyful Mysteries
1. The Annunciation
2. The Visitation
3. The Nativity
4. The Presentation in the Temple
5. The Finding of Jesus in the Temple

Mysteries of Light
1. Jesus' Baptism in the Jordan River
2. Jesus' Self-Manifestation at the Wedding of Cana
3. The Proclamation of the Kingdom of God and Jesus' Call to Conversion
4. The Transfiguration
5. The Institution of the Eucharist at the Last Supper

Sorrowful Mysteries
1. The Agony in the Garden
2. The Scourging at the Pillar
3. The Crowning with Thorns
4. The Carrying of the Cross
5. The Crucifixion

Glorious Mysteries
1. The Resurrection
2. The Ascension
3. The Descent of the Holy Spirit

4. The Assumption of Mary

5. The Crowning of Mary as the Queen of Heaven and Earth

How to Pray the Rosary
Opening

1. Begin on the crucifix and pray the Apostles' Creed.

2. On the first bead, pray the Our Father.

3. On the next three beads, pray the Hail Mary. (Some people meditate on the virtues of faith, hope, and charity on these beads.)

4. On the fifth bead, pray the Glory Be.

The Body

Each decade (set of ten beads) is organized as follows:

1. On the larger bead that comes before each set of ten, announce the mystery to be prayed (see above) and pray one Our Father.

2. On each of the ten smaller beads, pray one Hail Mary while meditating on the mystery.

3. Pray one Glory Be at the end of the decade. (There is no bead for the Glory Be.)

Conclusion

Pray the following prayer at the end of the rosary:

Hail, Holy Queen (see page 135)

Chaplet of Divine Mercy

The Chaplet of Divine Mercy is a devotion based on the visions of St. Mary Faustina Kowalska, a Polish sister canonized in 2000. This is a rosary-based devotion you can recite with rosary beads or by counting the prayers on your fingers.

1. Starting on the crucifix, make the Sign of the Cross.

2. Say three times: "O Blood and Water, which gushed forth from the Heart of Jesus as a fountain of Mercy for us, I trust in Thee!"

3. Pray the Our Father.

4. Pray the Hail Mary.

5. Recite the Apostles' Creed.

6. Say the following: "Eternal Father, I offer you the Body and Blood, Soul and Divinity, of your dearly beloved Son, Our Lord Jesus Christ, in atonement for our sins and those of the whole world."

7. On the ten small beads say: "For the sake of his sorrowful Passion, have mercy on us and on the whole world."

8. Repeat steps 6 and 7 for all five decades.

9. Conclude by saying three times: "Holy God, Holy Mighty One, Holy Immortal One, have mercy on us and on the whole world."

Stations of the Cross

The Stations of the Cross are individual pictures or symbols hung on the interior walls of most Catholic churches depicting fourteen steps along Jesus' way of the cross. Praying the stations means meditating on each of the following scenes:

1. Jesus is condemned to death.

2. Jesus takes up his cross.

3. Jesus falls the first time.

4. Jesus meets his Mother.

5. Simon of Cyrene helps Jesus carry his cross.

6. Veronica wipes the face of Jesus.

7. Jesus falls the second time.

8. Jesus consoles the women of Jerusalem.

9. Jesus falls the third time.

10. Jesus is stripped of his garments.

11. Jesus is nailed to the cross.

12. Jesus dies on the cross.

13. Jesus is taken down from the cross.

14. Jesus is laid in the tomb.

Some churches also include a fifteenth station, the Resurrection of the Lord.

Litany of Humility

O Jesus, meek and humble of heart, Hear me.
From the desire of being esteemed, Deliver me,
    O Jesus.
From the desire of being loved, Deliver me, O Jesus.
From the desire of being extolled, Deliver me,
    O Jesus.
From the desire of being honored, Deliver me,
    O Jesus.
From the desire of being praised, Deliver me,
    O Jesus.

From the desire of being preferred to others,
  Deliver me, O Jesus.

From the desire of being consulted, Deliver me,
  O Jesus.

From the desire of being approved, Deliver me,
  O Jesus.

From the fear of being humiliated, Deliver me,
  O Jesus.

From the fear of being despised, Deliver me,
  O Jesus.

From the fear of suffering rebukes, Deliver me,
  O Jesus.

From the fear of being calumniated, Deliver me,
  O Jesus.

From the fear of being forgotten, Deliver me,
  O Jesus.

From the fear of being ridiculed, Deliver me,
  O Jesus.

From the fear of being wronged, Deliver me,
  O Jesus.

From the fear of being suspected, Deliver me,
  O Jesus.

That others may be loved more than I, Jesus, grant
  me the grace to desire it.

That others may be esteemed more than I, Jesus,
  grant me the grace to desire it.

That, in the opinion of the world, others may
  increase and I may decrease, Jesus, grant me the
  grace to desire it.

That others may be chosen and I set aside, Jesus,
   grant me the grace to desire it.
That others may be praised and I go unnoticed,
   Jesus, grant me the grace to desire it.
That others may be preferred to me in everything,
   Jesus, grant me the grace to desire it.
That others may become holier than I, provided
   that I may become as holy as I should, Jesus, grant
   me the grace to desire it.

NOVENAS

A novena consists of the recitation of certain prayers over nine days. The symbolism of nine days refers to the time Mary and the Apostles spent in prayer between Jesus' Ascension into Heaven and Pentecost.

Many novenas are dedicated to Mary or a saint, with the faith and the hope that she or he will intercede for the one making the novena. Novenas to St. Jude, St. Anthony, Our Lady of Perpetual Help, and Our Lady of Lourdes remain popular in the Church today.

The Divine Praises

These praises are traditionally recited after the Benediction of the Blessed Sacrament:

   Blessed be God.
   Blessed be his holy name.
   Blessed be Jesus Christ, true God and true man.
   Blessed be the name of Jesus.
   Blessed be his most Sacred Heart.
   Blessed be his most Precious Blood.
   Blessed be Jesus in the most holy sacrament of the altar.

Blessed be the Holy Spirit, the Paraclete.
Blessed be the great Mother of God, Mary most holy.
Blessed be her holy and Immaculate Conception.
Blessed be her glorious Assumption.
Blessed be the name of Mary, Virgin and Mother.
Blessed be Saint Joseph, her most chaste spouse.
Blessed be God in his angels and his saints.

PRAYERS

Some common Catholic prayers are listed below. The Latin translation for three of the prayers is included. Latin is the official language of the Church. There are several occasions when you may pray in Latin, for example, at a World Youth Day when you are with young people who speak different languages.

Sign of the Cross

In the name of the Father,
and of the Son,
and of the Holy Spirit.
Amen.

In nómine Patris,
et Filii,
et Spíritus Sancti.
Amen.

Our Father

Our Father
who art in heaven,
hallowed be thy name.
Thy kingdom come;

thy will be done on earth as it is in heaven.
Give us this day our daily bread
and forgive us our trespasses
as we forgive those who trespass against us.
And lead us not into temptation,
but deliver us from evil.
Amen.

Pater Noster qui es in caelis:
sanctificétur Nomen Tuum;
advéniat Regnum Tuum;
fiat volúntas Tua,
sicut in caelo, et in terra.
Panem nostrum
cotidiánum da nobis hódie;
et dimítte nobis débita nostra,
sicut et nos
dimíttimus debitóribus nostris;
Et ne nos inducas in tentatiónem,
sed libera nos a Malo.
Amen.

Glory Be

Glory be to the Father
and to the Son
and to the Holy Spirit,
as it was in the beginning,
is now,
and ever shall be,
world without end.
Amen.

Win ^{it} All

Glória Patri
et Filio
et Spiritui Sancto.
Sicut erat in princípio,
et nunc et semper,
et in sae'cula saeculórum.
Amen.

Hail Mary

Hail Mary, full of grace,
the Lord is with thee.
Blessed art thou among women
and blessed is the fruit of thy womb, Jesus.
Holy Mary, Mother of God,
pray for us sinners now
and at the hour of our death.
Amen.

Ave, María, grátia plena,
Dóminus tecum.
Benedicta tu in muliéribus,
et benedíctus fructus ventris
tui, Iesus.
Sancta María, Mater Dei,
ora pro nobis peccatoribus
nunc et in hora mortis nostrae.
Amen.

Memorare

Remember, O most gracious Virgin Mary,
that never was it known
that anyone who fled to your protection,

implored your help,
or sought your intercession was left unaided.
Inspired by this confidence,
I fly unto you,
O virgin of virgins, my Mother,
To you I come, before you I stand,
sinful and sorrowful.
O Mother of the Word incarnate,
despise not my petitions,
but in your mercy hear and answer me.
Amen.

Hail, Holy Queen

Hail, holy Queen, Mother of Mercy,
our life, our sweetness, and our hope!
To you do we cry,
poor banished children of Eve;
to you do we send up our sighs,
mourning and weeping in this valley of tears.
Turn then, O most gracious advocate,
your eyes of mercy toward us,
and after this exile,
show us the blessed fruit of your womb, Jesus.
O clement, O loving, O sweet Virgin Mary.
V. Pray for us, O holy mother of God.
R. that we may be made worthy of the promises of
   Christ. Amen.

The Angelus

V. The angel spoke God's message to Mary.
R. And she conceived by the Holy Spirit.

Win it All

Hail Mary . . .

V. Behold the handmaid of the Lord.

R. May it be done unto me according to your word.

Hail Mary . . .

V. And the Word was made flesh.

R. And dwelled among us.

Hail Mary . . .

V. Pray for us, O holy mother of God.

R. That we may be made worthy of the promises of Christ.

Let us pray: We beseech you, O Lord, to pour out your grace into our hearts. By the message of an angel we have learned of the Incarnation of Christ, your Son; lead us by his Passion and cross, to the glory of the resurrection. Through the same Christ our Lord. Amen.

Regina Caeli

Queen of heaven, rejoice, alleluia.

The Son you merited to bear, alleluia,

has risen as he said, alleluia.

Pray to God for us, alleluia.

V. Rejoice and be glad, O Virgin Mary, alleluia.

R. For the Lord has truly risen, alleluia.

Let us pray.

God of life, you have given joy to the world by the resurrection of your Son, our Lord Jesus Christ. Through the prayers of his mother, the Virgin Mary, bring us to the happiness of eternal life. We ask this through Christ our Lord. Amen.

Prayer of St. Michael the Archangel

St. Michael, the Archangel, defend us in battle. Be
our safeguard against the wickedness and snares of
the devil. May God rebuke him, we humbly pray;
and do you, O Prince of the heavenly host, by the
power of God cast into hell Satan and all the evil
spirits who wander through the world seeking the
ruin of souls. Amen.

Grace at Meals

Before Meals
Bless us, O Lord,
and these, your gifts,
which we are about to receive from your bounty,
through Christ our Lord. Amen.

After Meals
We give you thanks, almighty God,
for these and all the gifts
which we have received
from your goodness
through Christ our Lord. Amen.

Guardian Angel Prayer

Angel of God, my guardian dear,
to whom God's love commits me here,
ever this day be at my side,
to light and guard, to rule and guide. Amen.

Prayer for the Faithful Departed

V.Eternal rest grant unto them, O Lord.
R. And let perpetual light shine upon them.

V. May their souls and the souls of all faithful
departed,

through the mercy of God, rest in peace.

R. Amen.

Morning Offering

O Jesus, through the immaculate heart of Mary,
I offer you my prayers, works, joys, and sufferings
of this day in union with the holy sacrifice of the
Mass throughout the world. I offer them for all
the intentions of your Sacred Heart: the salvation
of souls, reparation for sin, the reunion of all
Christians. I offer them for the intentions of our
bishops and all members of the apostleship of
prayer and in particular for those recommended by
your Holy Father this month. Amen.

Act of Faith

O God,

I firmly believe all the truths that you have revealed
and that you teach us through your Church,

for you are truth itself

and can neither deceive nor be deceived.

Amen.

Act of Hope

O God,

I hope with complete trust that you will give me,
through the merits of Jesus Christ, all necessary
grace in this world

and everlasting life in the world to come,

for this is what you have promised

and you always keep your promises.

Amen.

Act of Love

O my God, I love you above all things, with my whole heart and soul, because you are all good and worthy of all my love. I love my neighbor as myself for the love of you. I forgive all who have injured me, and I ask pardon of all whom I have injured. Amen.

Act of Contrition

O my God, I am heartily sorry for having offending Thee, and I detest all my sins because of thy just punishments, but most of all because they offend Thee, my God, who art all good and deserving of all my love. I firmly resolve with the help of Thy grace to sin no more and to avoid the near occasion of sin. Amen.

GOING TO MASS

The "obligation" to attend Sunday Mass is rooted in the law of the Lord and expressed in the Third Commandment. Participating at Mass helps us celebrate Christ's resurrection. In addition, Sundays are to be days when we relax and unwind from the week, spend time with family, and avoid unnecessary work.

Like the Sunday obligation, we are to attend Mass on specially designated holy days. In the United States, these are:

- Feast of the Immaculate Conception (December 8)
- Christmas (December 25)

- Solemnity of Mary (January 1)
- Feast of the Ascension (when celebrated on a Thursday, forty days after Easter)
- Assumption of Mary (August 15)
- All Saints' Day (November 1)

MORE FAVORITE PRAYERS
Five-Minute Prayer
(inspired by a lesson Fr. Larry Richards taught me in high school)

> For one minute, share with the Lord what you are sorry for.
> For one minute, share with the Lord what you are thankful for.
> For one minute, share with the Lord the people who asked you to pray for them.
> For one minute, surrender your life to the Lord.
> For one minute, listen to the Lord in silence.

I Give You My Life Prayer
(I prayed this prayer with many future saints from Paramus Catholic High School)

> Lord Jesus, I give you my life through pain, suffering, and through joy. (Repeat five times.)

Mary the Mother of God Surrender Prayer
(taught to me by Greg Schlueter)

> I am your suffering servant; be it done unto me according to your word. (Repeat three times.)

KNOW YOUR BIBLE

He said to them in reply, "It is written:
'One does not live by bread alone
but by every word that comes forth
from the mouth of God.'" (Mt 4:4)
At a young age, I learned that memorizing and knowing God's Word was vital to being the best Christian you can be. To live an adult faith, you need to know God's Word by heart. Start by memorizing these verses:

We know that all things work for good for those who love God, who are called according to his purpose.
Romans 8:28

Everything is possible to the one who has faith.
Mark 9:23

For God so loved the world that he gave his only Son so that everyone who believes in him might not perish but might have eternal life.
John 3:16

If you confess with your mouth that Jesus is Lord and believe in your heart that God raised him from the dead, you will be saved.
Romans 10:9

I came so that they might have life and have it more abundantly.
John 10:10

STEPS TO WINNING IT ALL

1: Recognize Your Importance

- Write letters of affirmation. _____

- Create an intercessory prayer list. _____

- Pray the Five-Minute Prayer (see page 140). _____

2: Discover Your Mission in Life

- Write your personal mission statement. _____

- Pray once a week with two or more people. _____

- Find a spiritual mentor to help you begin to discern your vocation. _____

3: Make Your Mess Your Message

- Write a letter about the lessons you have learned from your messes. _____

- Seek forgiveness from someone you have caused pain. _____

- Make a commitment to go to confession at least once a month. _____

4: Keep Your Passion

- Find a service project to be involved with. _____

- Be passionate about your life story and share it with others. _____

- Pick one sin that is giving you a hard time and eliminate it. _____

5: Remain Fearless

- Write down five personal fears and share   _____
  them with your mentor.

- Take a stand for a person in your life who   _____
  is being dissed.

- Encourage one person who intimidates you.   _____

6: Commit to Loving

- Reserve time for prayer and adoration before   _____
  the Blessed Sacrament.

- Spend at least five minutes daily listening to   _____
  God speak to you.

- Name your enemies and then pray for them.   _____

7: Never Give Up

- Watch a movie with a positive, inspiring message. _____

- Call on those who have encouraged your faith   _____
  and thank them.

- Begin each day with Christ by praying the   _____
  Morning Offering (see page 138).

8: Live Every Day as If It Were Your Last

- Recite the Mary the Mother of God   _____
  Surrender Prayer daily (see page 140).

- Meditate with the crucifix on Christ's love for you. _____

- Set a regular day from Monday to Friday   _____
  to go to Mass.

A Special Acknowledgment

I would like to thank some of the priests who have blessed my life over the years. Without the time and energy each of you spent with me, I do not even know where I would be. I wrote this book in the Year of the Priest. Thank you for inspiring me to be a leader. It is because of all of you that I am the man I am today.

Fr. Lou Aiello

Msgr. William Biebel

Msgr. Paul Bochicchio

Fr. Leo Butler

Fr. Fred Byrne

Msgr. James Cafone

Fr. Peter Cameron, O.P.

Fr. Justin Capota, O.S.B.

Bishop Thomas Costello

Fr. John Detisch

Fr. Mike Donovan

Fr. Mitch Doyen

Fr. Hugh Vincent Dyer, O.P.

Fr. Tom Elewaut, C.J.

Fr. Joseph Espaillat

Fr. John Fenlon

Fr. John Gordon

Fr. Kevin Gugliotta

Fr. Bill Halbing

Fr. Kevin Hanbury

Fr. Jerry Hayes

Fr. Mark Hoffman

Fr. Mike Joly

Fr. Jon Kalisch, O.P.

Fr. Tim Klosterman

Fr. Brian Lang

Msgr. Richard Liddy

Fr. Ed Lohse

Fr. Jerome Macher, O.C.S.O.

Fr. John Manno

Fr. Michael McCormick

Fr. Bob Meyers

Msgr. Thomas Nydegger

Fr. Joseph O'Connor

Cardinal Seán O'Malley,
    O.F.M. Cap.

Fr. Bryan Page

Fr. John Paladino

Fr. Henry Pedzich

Msgr. Sabato Pilato

Fr. Richard Prior

Fr. Willy Raymond, C.S.C.

Fr. Peter Reddick

Bishop Kevin Rhoades

Fr. Larry Richards

Fr. Nick Rouch

Fr. Jude Salus, O.S.B.

Msgr. Robert Sheeran

Fr. Bill Sheridian

Msgr. John Slater

Fr. Jim Spera

Fr. Rich Toohey

Msgr. Lloyd Torgerson

Fr. Agostino Torres, C.F.R.

Bishop Donald Trautman

Fr. Marc Vicari

A POEM
for Catherine called "Gigi and B"

You will die and so will I. Pretty intense to say, as you, my daughter,
     are only two.
Yes, that is true, and so important as I write this poem for you.
You are just on loan from a Father in Heaven,
who gave his son Jesus Christ to die for our sin.
I need to live as a Father who only cares about what will happen when
     it all ends,
in hopes that our savior, Jesus, will call us his friends.
When someone dies we think long and hard about why?
When someone like Gigi dies I will know why they cried.
B, listen to your Daddy when I say, Gigi did live a life of loving her faith
     all the way so you would undoubtedly be okay.
I sit here as I pray, thinking of you and Gigi.
Ninety years separate you, just a blink in God's eye, remembering life
     is short is the key.
B is in need and so is Gigi,
They are pure-hearted and loving to a tee.
Winning it all is what reminds me of what I want for you, B, and all
     those I meet.
Beauty is fleeting, time is short, but one thing I desire for my little B,
that you will win it all like Gigi taught her family.
Gigi cared for what mattered and valued what was true.
Her simple faith in God, I could see was so pure.
Remember B, putting faith in God, we having nothing to lose.
You are so little now, how could you be big?
How I wish you would always be just a kid.
Time will go fast and one day I will walk you down the aisle,
I hope the faith handed down to you will be cherished through
     each mile.
I love you B and I am so thankful to God for your mom, Mary's
     grandma, Gigi.

She has laid the foundation that faith is our number one necessity.
To the world Gigi is dying,
but to those who know the Risen Christ she is living.
So B, whenever you lose focus and think you've lost your way
just ask about Gigi and what mattered to her, and everything will
    be okay.
Gigi loved Christ, cherished Mass daily like Lombardi, and prayed
    the Rosary.
That's winning it all dear Catherine and don't forget the mission Gigi
    laid before you.
Please just say yes to the Call
that was started by my dear friend St. Paul.
No time for games, choose it today!
We need to win it all, we don't have time to waste.
Be a sister, be married, be single, it's up to you.
But never forget what holds the world together, and that's God's love,
    you silly goose!

Love You B,
    Daddy

Justin Fatica is the cofounder of Hard as Nails Ministries, which has had an impact on millions across the globe. Fatica and other lay and ordained ministers from Hard as Nails speak regularly at evangelical music festivals, diocesan youth conferences, confirmation retreats, school assemblies, graduations, youth group meetings, days of recollection, prisons, parish missions, and more.

Fatica has also delivered keynote addresses and witnessed to the power of the Gospel at Sunday Masses, amusement parks, and athletic events. His ministry was the subject of an HBO documentary that allowed the world to know Fatica as an intense, controversial, passionate, and genuine minister. He has also been featured on *Good Morning America*, *Nightline*, Sirius Radio and more. Fatica went to Seton Hall University and holds a bachelor's degree in elementary education and philosophy and a master's degree in education. He taught high school theology at Paramus Catholic High School in New Jersey.

He is also the cofounder of The Stand, an adult seminar series designed to motivate business leaders, educators, and parents to empower others. In 2009, Fatica's first book, *Hard as Nails*, a chronicle of his life and ministry, was published by Doubleday, and his speaking schedule included such highlights as The Awakening, Soulfest, and the Los Angeles Religious Education Congress. He currently lives in Syracuse, New York, with his wife Mary and two children.

Founded in 1865, Ave Maria Press,
a ministry of the Congregation of
Holy Cross, is a Catholic publishing
company that serves the spiritual and
formative needs of the Church and its
schools, institutions, and ministers;
Christian individuals and families; and
others seeking spiritual nourishment.

For a complete listing of titles from

Ave Maria Press

Sorin Books

Forest of Peace

Christian Classics

visit www.avemariapress.com

ave maria press® / Notre Dame, IN 46556
A Ministry of the Indiana Province of Holy Cross